DATE DUE			

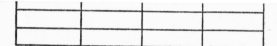

For Reference

Not to be taken from this room

Organized Labor
in New Jersey

THE NEW JERSEY HISTORICAL SERIES

Edited by

RICHARD M. HUBER   WHEATON J. LANE

The New Jersey Historical Series

Supplementary Volume

Organized Labor

in New Jersey

LEO TROY

1965

D. VAN NOSTRAND COMPANY, INC.

Princeton, New Jersey

New York, N. Y. • Toronto, Canada • London, England

788382-9

D. VAN NOSTRAND COMPANY, INC.
120 Alexander St., Princeton, New Jersey (*Principal office*)
24 West 40 Street, New York 18, New York

D. VAN NOSTRAND COMPANY, LTD.
358, Kensington High Street, London, W.14, England

D. VAN NOSTRAND COMPANY (*Canada*), LTD.
25 Hollinger Road, Toronto 16, Canada

Published simultaneously in Canada by
D. VAN NOSTRAND COMPANY (Canada), LTD.

PRINTED IN THE UNITED STATES OF AMERICA

FOREWORD

Many tracks will be left by the New Jersey Tercentenary celebration, but few will be larger than those made by the New Jersey Historical Series. The Series is a monumental publishing project—the product of a remarkable collaborative effort between public and private enterprise.

New Jersey has needed a series of books about itself. The 300th anniversary of the State is a fitting time to publish such a series. It is to the credit of the State's Tercentenary Commission that this series has been created.

In an enterprise of such scope, there must be many contributors. Each of these must give considerably of himself if the enterprise is to succeed. The New Jersey Historical Series, the most ambitious publishing venture ever undertaken about a state, was conceived by a committee of Jerseymen—Julian P. Boyd, Wesley Frank Craven, John T. Cunningham, David S. Davies, and Richard P. McCormick. Not only did these men outline the need for such an historic venture; they also aided in the selection of the editors of the series.

Both jobs were well done. The volumes speak for themselves. The devoted and scholarly services of Richard M. Huber and Wheaton J. Lane, the editors, are a part of every book in the series. The editors have been aided in their work by two fine assistants, Elizabeth Jackson Holland and Bertha DeGraw Miller.

To D. Van Nostrand Company, Inc. my special thanks for recognizing New Jersey's need and for bringing their skills and publishing wisdom to bear upon the printing and distributing of the New Jersey Historical Series.

My final and most heartfelt thanks must go to Leo Troy, who accepted my invitation to write *Organized Labor in New Jersey,* doing so at great personal sacrifice and without thought of material gain. We are richer by his scholarship. We welcome this important contribution to an understanding of our State.

January, 1965

RICHARD J. HUGHES
Governor of the
State of New Jersey

PREFACE

This volume in the New Jersey Historical Series is the first general survey of the labor movement of New Jersey. It is a subject which has hitherto been neglected not only in this state, but in other leading industrial states as well. Yet without these accounts, the significance of national movements cannot be properly weighed and evaluated. They are either exaggerated or undervalued. For example, the importance of the national union movement from 1861 to 1873, so widely stressed in the standard histories, seems much less important when seen from New Jersey's experience. On the other hand, the impact of the Knights of Labor on the formation of state and local associations, and on the formation of unions themselves appears far more important than is usually credited, again based on New Jersey's experience. The new perspectives suggested by the union history in this state deserve serious consideration since the distinguishing characteristic of the rise of organized labor in New Jersey in its representative quality. No major national development failed to leave an imprint in this state. From the movement to free labor markets and the first labor organizations to the founding of the American Federation of Labor and Congress of Industrial Organizations, New Jersey labor has been involved.

The State's balance of industry and employment, not too dissimilar from the nation's probably has made it representative of the development of unions. Its strategic position between New York and Philadelphia may have enabled the State to benefit from the germination of new ideas and movements and become a testing ground of their future evolution. Thus, the founding of the New Jersey State Labor Congress in 1879, forerunner of the State Federation of Labor, AFL, tested and proved one of the earliest state federations.

New Jersey, too, seems to reflect some of the national mood, difficulties, and drawbacks of organized labor in this country. The merger of the American Federation of Labor with the Congress of Industrial Organizations was accomplished nationally at the end of 1955. In New Jersey, the merger took six more years, making the state the last in which the unions united. In June, 1964, the two wings of the State AFL-CIO broke apart and the issue which tipped the scales and sundered the newly merged group was one which bedevils the nation and the national labor movement—civil rights.

Wholesale differences in philosophy, methods, origin, and personalities widen the division within the state. What does all this portend? Is New Jersey's reconstituted CIO (formally still within the state and national associations) to become the national pattern for all disaffected branches of the AFL-CIO?

Corrupt leadership in parts of the national union movement has its counterparts in New Jersey. Corruption has been a problem and continues to vitiate the effectiveness and image of organized labor in both state and national settings.

On the other hand, Communist domination of unions, principally a CIO problem in the past, has been virtually eliminated in the country and in this state. Indeed, the leadership of the New Jersey State CIO was in the forefront of the move to eliminate the Party and its followers from the union movement.

New Jersey's union movement also mirrors the nation's in the loss of members and the decline in the proportion of the work force organized. While its economic and political power remain strong, we believe the state and national movements have passed their crest of power.

Typically in studies of labor movements, one or more individuals stand out and give it direction and color.

◂§ x §▸

Their ideals, aspirations, and great energy impart an organizational image—and often fuel its drive. However, in our study, we have emphasized organizations rather than individuals, not arbitrarily, but because not one in the history of the New Jersey union movement dominated it or gave it a philosophy in the manner of Samuel Gompers, John L. Lewis, Sidney Hillman, Philip Murray, George Meany, or Walter Reuther. If anything, we believe that historically the leaders of the various New Jersey labor organizations were all effective organizational men. Their philosophical orientation usually reflected the prevailing theories, while their local purposes were intertwined with those of the organizations they served. If the individuals were separated from the organizations, the organizations might well have operated less efficiently, but function they would.

In 1964, about 760,000 persons, or one out of every 20 union members in the United States worked in New Jersey. The unions represented about one-third of the non-farm employees of the state. The purpose of this study is to record and explain how the union movement of New Jersey reached this stage of development.

This study owes much to a large number of people both in and out of the labor movement. Foremost is the debt I owe Miss Miriam Studley of the Newark Public Library. In addition, I wish to acknowledge the cooperation and help of Donald Sinclair, Rutgers University Library, Mr. Joel Jacobson, President of the New Jersey State Industrial Union Council, Mr. Vincent J. Murphy, President of the New Jersey State AFL-CIO, Harry Burke, of the *Newark Evening News,* my colleague, Professor Thomas Reynolds, and my student assistant, Mr. Allan Wahler.

Others whose contributions were significant are former Governor Robert Meyner, James Merrit, and Gilbert Cohen of the Newark College of Arts and Sciences Library, Thomas Kean, Public Relations Director of the AFL-CIO, Thomas Parsonnet, its Chief Counsel, Anthony Nicolosi of the Rutgers University Library, Mrs.

Maud Pech of the National Bureau of Economic Research for statistical and chart work, and Thomas Gallagher, whom I didn't meet, but whose trenchent columns in the *Newark Star Ledger* were very helpful. My thanks, too, to Miss Jenifer Thompson for her typing. To the editors of the Tercentenary Series, Dick Huber and Wheaton Lane, my appreciation for their help in bringing this volume to publication. To my wife, Sandra, and my children, Alex and Suzannah, my gratitude for their forbearance. For what is written here, I alone am responsible.

LEO TROY

Newark, New Jersey
December, 1964

TABLE OF CONTENTS

❦ xiii ❧

LIST OF ILLUSTRATIONS

LIST OF TABLES AND CHARTS

I

FROM REGULATED TO FREE
LABOR

Trade unions arose in New Jersey and the Nation with the development of markets governed by supply and demand. In America, this occurred by the end of the eighteenth century, but the first known union in New Jersey came a little after the turn of the century.

From Colonial times to the early national period, public authorities regulated employment, hours, rates of pay, and related terms of work, and until these regulations were largely abandoned, the economic conditions necessary for the appearance of trade unions did not exist.

The controls to which labor was subject were a key part of a general system of economic regulation known as national mercantilism. National mercantilism was, therefore, an economic philosophy opposed to the philosophy of laissez faire which came to the forefront in America and Britain at the end of the eighteenth century and remains to this day the economic philosophy of our country.

Colonial Regulation

British economic policy in the colonies favored the political and military power of the home country. Foreign markets were to be penetrated and expanded while imports were to be carefully restricted. Tariffs protected domestic industry and bounties stimulated exports. A favorable balance of payments and the acquisition of precious metals measured success. Imperial exploitation of colonies, especially the American colonies, was of central importance to the expansion of foreign trade: colonies would become suppliers of raw materials and consumers of Britain's finished products.

The keystone of the system was the regulated labor market. To be a worker under this system was to be a small cog in the large machine of the State.

Mercantilist rules for labor were expressed in the Tudor Statute of of Apprentices (1563), Poor Laws (1601), and later the Acts of Settlement (1662). These were carried to the American colonies, but neither the free colonial laborer nor the colonial entrepreneur became as closely bound by them as his counterparts in England. The geographic distances between colonies, the absence of centralized political control, and continuous immigration all contributed to this difference. From the beginning, then, Americans have always had less governmental regulation of their economic lives than Europeans and Britons.

The colonial versions of mercantilist regulations also differed in degree and substance among the colonies. Massachusetts' authorities applied the rules most broadly and strictly, while New Jersey's rules were moderate. Typically the labor "codes" enacted by colonial legislatures, towns, and other political units provided for compulsory labor, restricted the movement of workers, governed apprenticeship, encouraged the employment of women and children, regulated discharges, and fixed wages—in short, embraced the entire labor market.

The colonies also began to regulate wages, and in New England, they were initially set by general legislation and made applicable throughout the colony. In New Jersey, by contrast, wage regulation was left to the various communities. Occupations "affected with a public interest" such as gravediggers, carmen, draymen, porters, chimney sweeps, and millers were commonly subject to regulation, and remained regulated for longer periods than others.

Control over wages necessarily required that the prices of products be controlled as well. Prohibitions on "forestalling" (buying futures in current parlance), "engrossing" (hoarding), "regrating" (purchasing at wholesale for retail sale), and monopolizing, which had their origins in medieval times, were common.

Because the colonists abhorred idleness and because labor was in short supply, the authorities, including those in New Jersey, required periods of compulsory labor at building and repairing roads, highways, and bridges. As near as possible, the burden was to be equally distributed among the inhabitants. Nevertheless, the rich were able to buy their way out. Those who failed to show up for duty were liable for the wages of substitutes, at times to double or treble the regular wages.

For example, the minutes of the Newark Town Meeting of June 10, 1669, state that:

It is ordered and agreed upon that the high Way through the Great Swamp shall be mended, and that those that have given in their Names to work at it shall work. . . . And in Case any man or men shall refuse to go when warned, without satisfying Reasons to the Surveyor, he or they shall have full Power to hire others in their room, though it be for double or treeble Wages.*

Local authorities could also draft and offer labor free of charge to induce businessmen to move into the area. In 1670, in an early example of area development, Newark offered three days of free labor from all men and women holding an allotment in the town to a group of businessmen in order to help set up a corn mill.

Workhouses which grew markedly in number into the mid-eighteenth century required vagrants, idlers, and rebellious children and servants to work. Frequently

* *Collections of The New Jersey Historical Society* (Newark, 1864), VI, 20.

this colonial version of convict labor became a cheap source of labor to privately owned businesses, particularly in such industries as textiles which could utilize low-cost, unskilled workers.

The movement of workers was also hedged about with numerous restrictions. Skilled workers, being in extremely short supply, were most restricted. They were prohibited from becoming farmers or tavern keepers, or even working in another colony until the needs of the home colony were met—and this was not likely to happen often.

To meet their needs for skilled workers, employers tapped all available sources of supply: free laborers, indentured persons, Negro slaves, as well as runaway indentured and slave labor. "Respectable" employers, like the son of Charles Reed, who operated an important iron foundry in Taunton, New Jersey, claimed,

> We have always made it an invariable rule at our Works never to be assistant in robing a Person of his Property by Secreating his Servant. The Contrary Conduct is base and unjust as well as ruinus to the Interest of the Iron Masters.*

As the occasion of these remarks, the younger Reed had been charged with employing a runaway indentured worker. The more reliable ironmasters were supposed to be bound by a code of honor not to induce workers to leave their employers nor to harbor them when they did.

Meanwhile, a vigorous policy was followed by both the British Government and the colonists of encouraging skilled workers to emigrate to America. However, just prior to the Revolutionary War, the British began to obstruct the flow of skilled workers.

New entrants to the skilled crafts were either trained as apprentices or brought into the colonial labor market

* Carl Raymond Woodward, "Charles Read of New Jersey and His Notes on Agriculture, 1715-1774," *Ploughs and Politicks* (New Brunswick, 1941), 91-92.

as immigrants. The Elizabethan Statute of Apprentices (1563) required seven years of training to become a carpenter, weaver, shipwright, or mason. The colonies followed this system, in general, but could never develop enough skilled manpower to meet their expanding needs.

An example of the workings of the apprentice system in New Jersey is an indenture contract between Pell Teed, a weaver, and his wife on the one hand, and the mother and step-father of one John Moris on the other. John Moris was to be apprenticed to Pell Teed to learn the trade of weaving, as well as to read and write, for a period of thirteen years and five months, or until he became twenty-one. (Apparently John's age was not definitely known.) During the years of his indenture, John was to follow a strict code of personal and business conduct, and his master and mistress were to supply him adequate food, clothing, and housing. On fulfillment of the agreement, John would be set free with a new suit of holiday clothes. In lieu of their inability to write their names, John's step-father, Thomas Force, and his mother Anny Force made their marks. The weaver and his wife both signed the agreement, the text of which follows:

This indenture witnesses that John Moris son to Stephen Moris deceast late of Newark in ye county of Essex and State of East Jersey hath of his own free will and accord and with ye full consent of his Father in Law Thomas Force and Mother Anne Force of Newark in said county put himself unto Pell Teed and Huma his wife of Newark in said county and with them after, as a servant and apprentice to serve and dwell for and during the term and space of thirteen years and five months or untill he shall arrive at ye age of twenty one years. During all which time ye said John his said Master and Mistress faithfully shall serve, their secrets keep, their lawfull commands gladly obey. He shal not absent himself by night or by day from ye servis of his said Master and Mistress without ye consent of his said Master and Mistress; at cards or dice or any other unlawfull games he shall not play whereby his said Master or Mistress shall have damage. With his own goods or ye goods of others he shall not trade or traffic to ye damage of his said Master or Mistress. He shall not commit fornification nor contract matrimony within ye said term of time nor frequent taverns or playhouses but in all things shall behave himself as a good and faithfull servant or apprentice ought during ye term aforesaid and ye said Master and Mistress shall procure and provide the said apprentice sutable and sufficient meat, drink, washing, lodging and apparel and learn him the weavers trade according to ye custom of ye country to do country work and learn him to read, write and cypher so as to keep book and at ye experation of said term of time to sett him free with one new suit of holiday cloaths and for a true performance the parties have hereunto interchangeably set their hands and seals this twenty fourth day of January one thousand seven hundred and seventy eight.

Signed sealed and delivered in the presence of
WILL'M ELY, LUCY PERKINS
Canoebrook

THOMAS X FORCE
ANNY X FORCE
PELL TEED
HUMA TEED *

Typical of the working life of an apprentice in the late eighteenth century are the experiences of "John Homespun," a pseudonym reminiscent of Benjamin Franklin's "Poor Richard," adopted by William Tuttle of New Vernon, New Jersey.**

In 1796, when he was fifteen years of age, William Tuttle was apprenticed in Newark in the printing trade. His master was a stern man whose authority was undisputed and for whom William and his fellow apprentices had little affection. Nor was his wife any more beloved by the young workmen.

After learning the alphabetical order of the type-case, he worked for weeks on end in applying the inks to the

---

* Photostatic copy belonging to Miriam Studley of Livingston.
**This brief account of his experiences is taken from the Rev. Joseph F. Tuttle, *The Life of William Tuttle* (New York, 1852).

types, a laborious task which made his arms ache. The Sunday rest was most welcome.

Needing spending money, William worked overtime, or what was then called "overwork." After finishing his daily labor as an apprentice he was allowed to fold books in the bindery, for which he was paid by the page. However, he was slow at "overwork" and could earn no more than five or six cents an evening. But the idea of earning perhaps a dollar a month kept him at it.

With the coming of winter and a lull in business during his first year as an apprentice, William was allowed to return home. His father interpreted this as an affront to himself and his son, so William Tuttle did not return to his apprenticeship in Newark.

Because of the persistent shortage of skilled labor, public regulation of occupational choice steadily relaxed throughout much of eighteenth-century America. But as laissez-faire policies spread, workers themselves began to request regulation of the labor market. Contrary to the system of mercantilist-inspired controls, however, workers were seeking laws to raise their wages. In a sense, the historical wheel had come full circle.

Thus, to limit competition, a group of weavers in New Jersey's Somerset County petitioned the legislature (without success) in 1772, "to prohibit Farmers and others from keeping looms in their Houses, and following the Weaving Business." *

Likewise, craftsmen sought to limit the geographic mobility of competitive labor as indicated by a petition of building tradesmen in New York to Governor De Witt Clinton requesting protection from an influx of workers from New Jersey who were undercutting their wage scales.**

The hiring of labor was also regulated, although the regulations on the demand side of the market were

* Richard B. Morris, *Government and Labor in Early America* (New York, 1946), 154.
** Richard B. Morris, *Government and Labor in Early America* (New York, 1946), 150.

apparently not so comprehensive as on the supply side. Workers under contract could not be dismissed without due cause and explanation to the authorities. Improper treatment would be cause for legal termination of an apprenticeship agreement in the crafts, professions, or sciences as late as 1798 under a New Jersey statute.* Disputes between the parties were subject to "mediation" followed by "compulsory arbitration." According to this act, if a justice of the peace could not settle the issue, he was then to call two other justices of the peace to join him as a court of arbitration whose decision would be binding.

In general, the workers' principal methods of obtaining redress prior to trade unionism were the courts or the slowdown. Neither was widely practiced or usually successful. However, public authorities discouraged the discharge of a worker when it would lead to his becoming a burden on the community as a recipient of poor relief.

There are examples of "severance" or dismissal pay being required of employers who discharged workers at seasons of the year when it might be difficult to find new employment. While New Jersey was governed by the Proprietors, masters were expected to furnish an indentured servant, at the expiration of his service, with two suits of apparel suitable for a former servant, one good felling axe, a good hoe, and seven bushels of Indian corn. In West Jersey, a servant's "severance pay" was ten bushels of corn, necessary apparel, two horses, and one axe.** In addition the courts in New Jersey consistently sought to curb employers who were cruel to their workers.

There was nothing comparable to a workmen's compensation law to cover workers injured in private em-

* "An Act respecting apprentices and servants, 14 March 1798," *Laws of the State of New Jersey*, compiled by W. Paterson (Blauvelt, 1800), 305-307.

** New Jersey Bureau of Statistics of Labor and Industry, *Eighth Annual Report, 1884*, 284.

ployment. However, neither was the employer free of responsibility for injuries to his employees which occurred on the job. In colonial times employers could be required to provide medical aid to injured employees, at least those who were under terms of indenture.

Unemployment resulting from technological change was a minor problem in the colonial period of New Jersey's and the Nation's history. There had been only small and limited advances in labor-saving devices; the size of the market and the scale of enterprise were too small to afford many opportunities for improving productive techniques. The typical production unit was a workshop with a few journeymen and apprentices. Joint stock companies were scarce and rarely found in industrial enterprises.

The principal non-farm industries in colonial New Jersey were iron mining and manufacturing, lumber and woodworking, leather, and flour manufacturing. New Jersey's ironworks became an important source of arms to the Revolutionary Army. The leading occupations associated with these industries were skilled; they included blacksmiths or farriers, wheelwrights, carpenters, millers, shoemakers, printers, masons, cabinetmakers, tanners, and bakers.

EMERGENCE OF FREE LABOR

Wars, economic development, and the legal concept of the free labor contract broke down eighteenth-century public controls over the employment relationship. At the same time these factors created a work force not only free of legal restraints, but one which identified its interests as separate and at times conflicting with those of the community and the employer.

The French and Indian War, 1756–1763, and the War of Independence dealt roughly with the tottering frame of colonial economic regulation. During both conflicts public authorities resorted heavily to the printing press to finance war needs. The magnification of money demand which ensued inflated prices rapidly and thereby tore at the foundations of economic control.

In the French and Indian War, for example, New Jersey raised the bulk of its financial contribution by the printing process. To mollify the Crown, New Jersey declared its paper money to be legal tender only in the Province. By 1760, it was reported that New Jersey's currency, though in better balance with its economy than Pennsylvania's or New York's, nevertheless had depreciated in value about 30 per cent.* Five years later, New Jersey had increased its deficit spending to nearly £350,-000 making its public debt the largest of any of the colonies.** Presumably, New Jersey's currency depreciated considerably more in the interim.

War finance during the Revolution repeated on a far larger scale the experience of the previous conflict. "Not worth a Continental" was a bitter measure of the devaluation of the currency.

Typically, prices of products, foodstuffs in particular, outran the rise in wages, so the workers' standard of living naturally fell. Attempts to restore a balance in prices by regulation failed. As "Rationalis," writing in the *New Jersey Gazette,* observed,

By the law lately passed for regulating prices, the legislature seem to have aimed at fixing most of the articles of internal produce at double the former prices. This may perhaps be a proper standard for some articles; but when the matter is fairly considered, it will be found that the same reasons which require the prices of some things to be doubled, will call for a similar advance on some others, and on others again a much greater. Of the latter kind are such articles as derive their value chiefly from labour, and require the use of some commodity, either imported from abroad, or which,

* Carl R. Woodward, *Ploughs and Politicks* (New Brunswick, 1941), 132, 133, 143.
** Richard P. McCormick, *New Jersey from Colony to State, 1609-1789* (Princeton, 1964), 72.

from it's scarcity, cannot be obtained but at a very high price.*

Nevertheless the efforts to establish and enforce controls went on through the War. And because they were ineffective, the wartime attempt to revive economic controls helped demolish regulation of labor markets. Despite their ineffectiveness, controls were popular during the War of Independence. In fact, New Jersey was one of the leading advocates of wartime economic regulation. In October, 1779, it joined New York in urging (unsuccessfully) that the Continental Congress impose economic controls.**

Within the state a large number of local committees were set up to prescribe and enforce regulations. In the summer of 1779, for example, a committee in Essex County set rates for transportation and for commodities at wholesale and retail at 14 times prices prevailing in 1774. In Burlington County, a committee set the wages of common labor, and fixed those of weavers, tailors, carpenters, and other mechanics employed on the materials of another at 16 times their rates of 1774. Violators would be "held up to the publick in a manner adequate to their offence." †

Although the War of Independence delivered the *coup de grâce* to mercantilist controls, the economic development of America had been undermining them for some time. Adam Smith's *The Wealth of Nations*, published in 1776, gave an economic explanation of a development already well underway in America, and stamped the movement toward laissez faire with an intellectual imprimatur.

Until the time of the Revolutionary War, markets

* Richard B. Morris, *Government and Labor in Early America* (New York, 1946), 129.
** Richard B. Morris, *Government and Labor in Early America* (New York, 1946), 113.
† Richard B. Morris, *Government and Labor in Early America* (New York, 1946), 113.

were continuously expanding to link up with those of adjoining communities, making regulation even in peacetime an increasingly difficult task. The newer markets were growing beyond the technical and political scope of local administrators.

The persistent shortage of skilled workers and the necessity of higher wages to attract labor contradicted the principle of fixing wage maximums, and although population increased rapidly—New Jersey's had risen from 61,000 in 1745 to well over 100,000 by the eve of the Revolution—the growth in demand for labor so far outstripped the supply that the regulatory system could not contain the mounting pressures.

The high wages prevailing in colonial America enabled many workmen to save enough to purchase farms, and, thereby, reduced the supply of industrial labor. Open lands and agricultural opportunities often attracted industrial labor, pushing wages upward and placing still more pressure on the weakening and increasingly irrational wage controls.

The higher income of American workmen must have contributed to the workers' indifference or opposition to regulation. Class attitudes were probably affected by the high standard of living and the upward social mobility American society has always afforded. Neither colonial workers, nor their successors were class conscious, and this accounts in great part for their acceptance of capitalism and their rejection of socialism. It is likely that some roots of this "classless" tradition originated in the material conditions of the colonial period. Doubtless, too, since many of immigrant workers had left their homelands to escape regulation, they would naturally oppose it in America as well.

Occupational differentiation and separation moved along with the growth of markets and the breakdown of public regulation. Capitalists became separated and distinct from wage earners. The gradual separation of occupational functions had become sufficiently clear by the eve of the Revolution so that it was possible for trade unions to emerge. And organizations for mutual assistance, friendly societies, did appear prior to the Revolution. However, judging from their character and operations, these organizations appear to be antecedents of trade unions. Like trade unions, they were organized on an occupational basis and provided sick and death benefits, but they included both masters and journeymen, which is rarely the case among unions.

There are a few examples of protests and strikes by workers, such as the strike of carpenters at the Hibernia Iron Works in New Jersey in 1774, but the workers' concerted action was not initiated by an organization and did not result in a permanent union.

Further sharpening of the economic differences between workers and employers was arrested by their joint response to British imperial policy in 1776. In this way, political or "national" interest arrested the rise of trade unions. The War intensified a feeling of "national solidarity," further sublimating the conflict of economic interests and, therefore of organization along economic lines. In the early national period, the economic conflicts re-appeared and the first well-established organizations of labor along with them.

In Newark, the demise of economic controls by the end of the War is reflected in advertisements for skilled labor. Thus, one Gerret Sickles advertised in 1781 for journeymen shoemakers, "who understood the making of boots, stuff shoes, etc. They will find constant employment and wages." *

The emergence of labor as a separate economic group is indicated by the report that in Newark's Fourth of July parade of 1788, "among the foremost marchers were cordwainers, (shoemakers), preceded by Mr. Plumb on a stage with four journeymen at work . . . with their tools." **

* Frank J. Urquart, *A History of the City of Newark* (New York, 1913), 503.
** Frank J. Urquart, *A History of the City of Newark* (New York, 1913), 503.

By the last decade of the eighteenth century governmental regulations of the labor market and the economy which had been brought to this country with the earliest settlements were largely displaced by the doctrine of laissez faire. As the network of controls was abandoned, labor and business soon began to emerge as separate answer to the problems of maintaining and improving their economic positions. For workers, the primary answer to the problems of manufacturing and improving living standards came to be the trade union. They did not eschew the possibility of laws to win their objectives, but their earliest efforts were usually rebuffed, as in the case of the weavers of Somerset County mentioned above.

In New Jersey, political recognition was given labor by the law of 1807 eliminating property qualification for voting. This amounted to political recognition of labor as an economic group within the state.

II

FORERUNNERS OF MODERN
UNIONS
1794-1860

Trade unions appeared in Newark probably within twenty years of their initial appearance in this country, an event which took place in Philadelphia in 1794. The Newark union, like the first one in Philadelphia, was of shoemakers.*

However, the Newark union did not last very long, apparently disbanding under the impact of the depression beginning in 1815 and lasting until 1820. Thereafter, from 1820 to about 1830, very few if any unions were formed in Newark or elsewhere in the state, although some Paterson workers in a Fourth of July celebration in 1823 declared: "May the mechanics of Paterson always feel themselves as independent of their employers as their employers are of them." **

Following the depression of 1827–1832, the tempo of union organization in New Jersey picked up. Unions appeared among shoemakers in Newark, Orange, Paterson, and New Brunswick. Unions were also organized

* The Webbs defined a trade union as "a continuous association of wage earners for the purpose of maintaining or improving the conditions of their working lives." Beatrice and Sidney Webb, *The History of Trade Unionism* (London, 1920), 1.

** Frank T. DeVyver, "The Organization of Labor in New Jersey Before 1860" (Unpublished doctoral dissertation, Princeton, 1934), 36.

among curriers (processors of hides for leather manufacture), saddlers and harness makers, tailors, carpenters, masons, painters, building laborers, stone cutters, and teamsters. Most of these were in Newark.

Among the various occupations and industries being organized in New Jersey, two stand out in this period: leather manufacturing and the building trades. By far the most active were the unions in leather processing. Among the shoemakers no less than three unions were known to have functioned in Newark in the early 1830's, the Union Benevolent Society of Journeymen Cordwainers, the Boot Makers Society, and the Journeymen Boot Fitters Society. Along with the unions of curriers and harness makers, the presence of these unions makes clear that at this time Newark was a leading center of leather manufacture.

The geographic scope of the first unions was the town or city, embracing as many employers as possible. Nearly all the unions were made up of skilled workers. How they were formed, carried out strikes, and prevented strike-breakers from taking their jobs is illustrated by the activities of the earliest union in America: the Federal Society of Cordwainers. Although a Philadelphia union, it had some members as far away as Trenton.*

From the record of a court case involving this union in 1806 we learn that whenever shoemakers came into town they soon learned via the grapevine, or were directly informed by members, that there was a union in the trade and that all were expected to join. Failure to join was "scabbing" and scabs were ostracized—or worse —by union members. One who did scab explained what it meant:

. . . no man would set upon the seat where I worked; that they would neither board or work where I was unless I joined. By a seat I mean they would not work in the same

* John R. Commons *et al.* (eds.), *A Documentary History of American Industrial Society* (New York, 1958), III, 79.

shop, nor board or lodge in the same house, nor would they work at all for the same employer.*

When the union struck they used roving picket lines, which were called "tramping committees," to keep non-union workers from the shop. Strike benefits were paid, provided there were funds. Allowances were half-a-dollar a week per dependent and the same for the striker.

GROWTH OF MARKETS AND CITIES

The year 1794 not only recorded the establishment of the first union but also the completion of the first turnpike in the United States, between Philadelphia and Lancaster, Pa. Thereafter, there were steady additions and improvements in the nations' transportation systems not only in roads, but also by means of canals, and in the introduction of the steamboat.

While the steamboat accelerated traffic generally in northerly-southerly directions, the canal-building program improved east-west communications. With the completion of the Erie Canal in 1825, and its immediate success, the east-west directional barrier to transportation began to give way. In New Jersey, the Morris Canal, 106 miles long, connected the Delaware River with Jersey City and thus linked the hinterland of Pennsylvania, via other canals, to the Port of New York. The Delaware and Raritan Canal, farther south, provided a similar connection; coal became its most important commodity of commerce.

But hardly had the canal system achieved its greatest successes when the railway age began, and the railways were to dominate American industrial development for the next century. Colonel John Stevens proved the mechanical feasibility of the steam railway on his estate

* John R. Commons *et al.* (eds.), *A Documentary History of American Industrial Society* (New York, 1958), III, 73.

in Hoboken in 1825. The construction of railways for commercial purposes began at about the turn of the third decade. From that time to the outbreak of the Civil War New Jersey increased its railway mileage from 61 miles of track in 1834 to 560 in 1860.* Railways soon diverted passenger traffic from the canals, but it was not until much later that the railways surpassed canals as the principal conveyance for freight as well.

Improvements in transportation stimulated the growth of towns and cities, but the spurt in urbanization in New Jersey did not come about until after 1820. This probably accounts for the slow start unions made in this state.

In 1810, Newark had some 4800 inhabitants and a decade later about 6500. By 1830, however, Newark's population had jumped to 11,000; and six years later, a census taken after it became an incorporated city reported nearly 20,000 persons. New Brunswick's population was 5900 in 1830. However, Paterson and Jersey City were not even listed as separate cities by the census in that year.

One of the industries earliest affected by the improvements in transportation and the growth of urbanization was shoemaking. Shoes were a major consumers' staple and were adaptable to market-production. Moreover, shoemaking did not undergo any important changes in manufacturing techniques until well into the nineteenth century. Without any means of improving workers' productivity, the competitive pressures on wages in the industry mounted with the continuing expansion of the market.

To the shoemaker of Newark, the spread of markets meant that employers "seemed determined to compel us to work for whatever sum they may stipulate, in order to undersell each other, or monopolize the whole business, or to be enabled thereby to live in luxury, while

* H. Wilson (ed.), *Outline History of New Jersey* (New Brunswick, 1950), 71.

those who work for them can scarcely obtain the common necessaries of life." *

Hat workers felt the same competitive pressures, but the pressures came to bear on them in different ways. For the hatters, the competition came about through the movement of workers from city to city, and from the sale of hats made abroad, particularly in England. Thus the Newark hat workers "resolved to stop 'itinerant' apprenticeship, as well as the admission of men too worthless or too unstable to remain in any other business," ** and to require a five-year apprenticeship, limit journeyman status to those twenty-one years of age or over, and to impose a closed shop, that is, require membership in the union as a condition of obtaining a job.

To meet the competition of English-made hats, the Journeymen Hatters of Newark declared their support of Henry Clay's American System, that is, for high tariffs: "We view," they said, "any attempt to lessen the existing duties on hats as directly tending to injure our trade, and that it is the duty of every journeyman hatter to express his opinion freely upon this subject, and to every exertion to protect this branch of American manufactures." † As a mark of esteem for Henry Clay, the Newark hatters presented him with a new hat.

Like the Journeymen Hatters, the Newark saddlers and harness makers had to meet foreign competition and therefore, like the hatters, they, too, supported a high tariff on their products. As a consequence of their support of high tariffs, many workers in New Jersey and

* Frank T. De Vyver, "The Organization of Labor in New Jersey Before 1860" (Unpublished doctoral dissertation, Princeton University, 1934), 20, quoting the *Newark Daily Advertiser*, April 26, 1836.

**Frank T. De Vyver, "The Organization of Labor in New Jersey Before 1860" (Unpublished doctoral dissertation, Princeton University, 1934), 56.

† Frank T. De Vyver, "The Organization of Labor in New Jersey Before 1860" (Unpublished doctoral dissertation, Princeton University, 1934), 53.

throughout the country supported Whig candidates rather than Democrats.

Printing was also affected by the movement of labor and therefore unions appeared early in this industry as well, except in New Jersey. It is puzzling that although there were numerous newspapers in the major towns of the state, the first printing union, an organization in Trenton, does not appear until after 1850. Moreover, it seems to have been formed as a result of the desire of the local printers to belong to the national union of printers then being organized. Unions of printers do not appear in Newark until about 1857, and in Jersey City until 1860.

The shoemakers' unions were the most active, at least as evidenced by the number of strikes they conducted. Shoe unions struck in Orange in 1832, again in 1835, in Newark in 1835 and 1836, and in Paterson in 1837. After a strike, a shoemakers' union in New Brunswick obtained a closed shop in 1836 when the employers agreed "not to give employment to any journeymen, except to a member of the Cordwainers Society of the City." *

Wages were the typical cause of strikes. Either employers sought to reduce them because of competition and business conditions, or unions wanted to raise them to meet increases in the cost of living.

In 1835, for example, a Newark shoeworkers' union struck because a wage demand to meet higher prices was refused: "It is well known," they said, "that our country is in a state of unparalleled prosperity. Money is plentiful; all the common necessaries of life have advanced in price; house rents have risen, in this place, from 10 to 30 per cent." **

* Frank T. DeVyver, "The Organization of Labor in New Jersey Before 1860" (Unpublished doctoral dissertation, Princeton University, 1934), 20, quoting the *Newark Daily Advertiser*, April 26, 1836.
** Frank T. DeVyver, "The Organization of Labor in New Jersey Before 1860" (Unpublished doctoral dissertation, Princeton University, 1934), 20-21, quoting the *Newark Daily Advertiser*, May 23, 1835.

In this strike the shoe union had the moral—and some material—support of other Newark trade unions and, most important of all, support of the city-wide association of unions formed a year earlier, the Newark Trades Union.

The Newark curriers struck in 1836 for higher wages. Later they joined curriers' unions in New York and Brooklyn in attempting to establish a uniform wage scale, but without success. The saddle and harness makers also struck in 1836. Their demand was higher wages. Building trades unions in Newark, Trenton, and New Brunswick joined in the rash of strikes in 1835-1836, to gain a shorter, ten-hour work day as well as to raise wages.

As a rule the strikes of this period were successful, at least in part, because times were prosperous—and indeed inflationary, what with an outpouring of notes by state banks.

Economists like Henry Vethake, Professor of Mathematics and Natural Philosophy at Queen's College (now Rutgers University) in 1813 and later Professor of Natural Philosophy at the College of New Jersey (Princeton), condemned the unions for striking to raise wages. In his *Principles of Political Economy* (1844), he declared that "no advantage can be derived, by the receivers of wages, from the trades' unions." He also stated:

Although . . . the action of the trades' unions can hardly be stigmatized as of a dishonest character, . ·. . such action is, nevertheless, a violation to a certain extent of the rights of property. And if these rights may be once violated by the trades' unions, they may be again and again violated by them; and the apprehension of this taking place would constitute a check to the accumulation of capital with its usual rapidity; inducing, in consequence, a fall of wages below the usual rate.

Consequently, trade unions are an unmixed evil causing inconvenience to capitalists, laborers, and consumers. Worst of all, according to Vethake,

they deny the notion maintained by political economists

that the natural course of things, of "free competition," is most conducive to the interest of both rich and poor. Instead, by their strikes to raise wages, they propagate the idea that a never-ceasing struggle of poor against rich is necessary to prevent the poor from being reduced to a bare subsistence.*

But even as they interfere with competition, the unions' efforts to raise wages are self-defeating, according to Vethake:

If the unions could raise wages permanently, this would outweigh all their disadvantages, for the prosperity of a people depends primarily on wages being high. But unions cannot do so because by reducing profits they retard capital accumulation.**

Vethake didn't expect his admonitions to be observed, but he at least hoped that his reasoning would reach "the evil-doers," and "those who had hastily given them encouragement on the ground that thereby they were contributing to the greatest good of the greatest number."

NEWARK TRADES UNION

The growth of the unions in Newark during the early 1830's led to the formation in 1834 of a city-wide federation of unions, the Newark Trades Union. It included unions from Orange and Paterson as well as Newark, and at its peak a total of 16 were associated, with a membership of nearly 1200. A similar federation was formed in New Brunswick in 1836. Thus, New Jersey had 2 of the 13 city associations operating in the country at this time.

The purpose of the Newark Trades Union, as stated in its constitution, was "to promote the general welfare

* Joseph Dorfman, *The Economic Mind in American Civilization* (New York, 1946), II, 736-737.
** Joseph Dorfman, *The Economic Mind in American Civilization* (New York, 1946), II, 737.

of Mechanics of the town of Newark, and to sustain their pecuniary interests." (Appendix A.)

Officers of the Newark Trades Union consisted of a president, vice-president, recording and corresponding secretary, treasurer and a finance committee. All were elected semi-annually by secret ballot. The constitution provided for regular monthly meetings with representation of affiliated unions based on their membership. Monthly dues were set at 6¼ cents per member.

Assistance to affiliated unions on strike was authorized only if the member union had been affiliated for at least six months, and if the strike had been authorized by two-thirds of the affiliated unions. Among those unions whose strikes were sanctioned by the Newark Trades Union were three Newark shoe unions, a hatters and a shoemakers union of Orange, and a carpenters union of Paterson.

New unions were admitted upon written application to the secretary and approval by a majority of the affiliated unions.

The constitution forbade the Newark Trades Union from considering or acting on political or religious issues.

From its statement of purpose, it is evident that the Newark Trades Union was one of the first labor associations in the country to rely on the economic or trade union approach to maintain and improve the living standards of its members. In this regard they anticipated the viewpoint of the American Federation of Labor founded more than half a century later.

Beside giving aid to its affiliated unions, the Newark association kept in touch with labor developments elsewhere in the country. The association entertained a group of Boston unionists visiting New Jersey in a campaign to enlist nation-wide support for a ten-hour day.

In the same year (1834) that the Newark unions set up their city association, they also sent delegates to New York to participate in forming a nation-wide association of local unions, the National Trades Union.

Newark delegates played a leading and Cassandra-like

role at the founding convention. A Newark shoemaker urged that the new National Trades Union concentrate on fostering unions in order to gain higher wages for workers, and to avoid involvement in politics. He argued that if the organization embraced politics it would eventually array one of the major political parties against labor to the disadvantage of the workers. His advice was "to organize and to improve their conditions." * However, the National Trades Union rejected the Newarker's advice and became deeply involved in politics.

The decision divided and weakened the new organization and contributed to its demise in the severe depression of 1837. Indeed, the depression was so deep that the Newark Trades Union, the New Brunswick Trades Union, and most of the local unions in New Jersey (and the country) succumbed.

Shoemakers' unions in New Jersey in the 1830's anticipated the future development of national unions. In 1835 they joined with shoe-workers from other cities and states in New York to establish a national organization in their trade. Among the 45 delegates were representatives from Newark, Elizabethtown, Rahway, Orange, Paterson, Bloomfield, Clinton, and New Brunswick. The first convention was, however, the last, as the organization foundered under the depression of 1837. It was just a little ahead of its time.

TEXTILE LABOR

About the time skilled workers in New Jersey's leading towns were forming unions in industries untouched by the industrial revolution, workers in the first industry to enter the machine age, cotton textiles, found themselves unable to organize unions. Indeed, over the next century, unionization continued to elude most of the

* E. B. Mittleman, "Trade Unionism," Part III in J. R. Commons *et al.* (eds.), *History of Labour in the United States* (New York, 1918), I, 426.

textile workers despite the best efforts of the workers themselves, business unionists, socialists, syndicalists, and communists.

The importance of cotton textiles in New Jersey dated from the early national period. The principal and, until the Civil War, virtually exclusive center was Paterson. Its proximity to water power and the types of water necessary for certain processes early marked Paterson as an advantageous locale for cotton textile production. The Society for the Establishment of Useful Manufactures promoted by Alexander Hamilton established one of the first mills in the town.

The industry came to rely heavily on low-wage female and child labor, because the machine made it possible to use unskilled women and children. Giving useful employment to children (whether consciously hypocritical or not) was in vogue. Free public education was, as yet, not available. Long hours were customary. As a result, labor relations were fraught with great potential stresses, which exploded into bitter and even bloody events. The dangers under these conditions are suggested by Sarah N. Cleghorn's lines:

> The golf links lie so near the mill
> That almost every day
> The laboring children can look out
> And see the men at play.

Child labor was used in New Jersey's cotton mills from the very beginning as indicated by the following excerpt from a letter written in 1794. A mill manager wrote to one of the directors and owners protesting frequent visits by ladies and gentlemen curious to see the new mill:

It will be proper to suggest to your consideration that parties of gentlemen and ladies should never on any pretence be admitted—it will be impossible to keep the children to their work whilst this is suffered, and the Society cannot afford to keep up such an establishment as a Show Shop.*

A report on employment in cotton spinning in Paterson around 1820 indicates the industry's heavy dependence on child labor: "From a calculation made by one of the manufacturers, it appears that there are 13 cotton spinning establishments with about 17,000 spindles, employing between 60 and 70 men, 50 or 60 women, and 600 children in the spinning departments alone.**

The skilled occupations, such as weaving, employed men and were organized from time to time, although not until late in the nineteenth century.

The first clash between Paterson textile employers and their employees began in 1828 over the issue of rescheduling the dinner hour from noon to one o'clock. It should be pointed out that the working day commenced about dawn and lasted until evening. Thus, there was a long stretch between breakfast and the midday meal.

The strike appears to be the first in the country involving factory operations. The strikers lost but received nation-wide publicity and sympathy. Probably as a result of the notoriety, the employers re-established the noon lunch hour.

A more serious struggle between employer and workers in cotton textiles occurred in 1835. A strike lasting six weeks and involving a reported 2000 people in 20 factories began on July 3, 1835, over the length of the working day, payment of wages in script, the withholding of one week's wages, fines for tardiness, and the contemptuous manner in which the employers treated representatives of the workers.

The principal demand was to reduce the working

* Letters of Peter Colt to Nicholas Low, 15 July 1794. Special Collections on New Jersey, Rutgers University, New Brunswick.
** Frank T. De Vyver, "The Organization of Labor in New Jersey Before 1860" (Unpublished doctoral dissertation, Princeton University, 1934), 140.

day. However, the actual hours themselves were in dispute. The workers claimed children worked 13½ hours; the employers, claimed it was, on average, 11½. The demand was for 11 hours, for 5 days of the week, and 9 on Saturday.

Whatever the actual hours, they were doubtless long as a comment on a suggestion to establish free schools at night for children and apprentices in the cotton mills brought out:

A night school would not benefit the mill hands inasmuch as they could not attend it—it is a well known fact that the children have to rise ere dawn of day, consume their morning meal by candle light and trudge to the mill to commence their labor ere the rising of the sun; at noon a very short time is allowed them for dinner, and their labor terminates at what is called 8 o'clock at night, but which is really (by the time they have their frames cleaned) much nearer 9 o'clock. They then take supper and immediately retire to bed in order that they may arise early in the morning—this being the mode of labor pursued in this and other manufacturing towns.*

The issues and the participants being what they were, the stoppage soon attracted wide attention (like the earlier strike) and developed bitter partisanship on both sides. Locally, the Newark Trades Union sent financial support and encouragement. It also formed a committee which it sent to Paterson to report on the strike. Workers' groups and unions also joined in sending relief and moral support. In New York, a meeting was held at Tammany Hall to raise money in support of the strikers.

The strike ended in a degree of compromise: 12 hours for the first 5 days and 9 on Saturdays. However, the children of parents who actively supported the strike were blacklisted. As for unions, none was established and the industry remained unorganized.

* Frank T. De Vyver, "The Organization of Labor in New Jersey Before 1860" (Unpublished doctoral dissertation, Princeton University, 1934), 145, quoting the *Courier*, Nov. 19, 1833.

Politics did interest workers, although unionists were often divided on the usefulness of the approach. In the period 1830 to 1837, workers and some unions carried on their political activities through newly organized political parties known as Workingmen's parties. However, these were not made up solely or even primarily of workers, nor did they espouse radical changes such as the abolition of private property. Professional men and small businessmen as well as workers belonged to the Workingmen's parties; their goals were social and political reform.

Three such parties were formed in Newark, one in 1830, another in 1834, and the last in 1836. They did not have a continuous existence nor, does it appear, did they enjoy the united backing of workers. Many workers believed their economic interests were more often parallel to their employers', particularly on the tariff question, and they so expressed themselves in letters to the local paper in Newark.

Some successes were scored in electing candidates by the Newark Workingmen's parties, but their impact was small by comparison with the Reform (or Workingmen's) Party of Trenton. The latter was active in a later period, from 1847 to 1860, but it pressed for the same issues previously demanded by the Workingmen's parties in Newark and, for that matter, in the country as a whole.

Among the leading reforms demanded were free public education, abolition of real property qualifications to hold office (real property ownership had not been a requisite for voting in the State since 1807); a 10-hour working day and greater limitations on the hours of child labor; exempting the first $200 or so of a debtor's property from seizure and sale, abolition of imprisonment for debt, a mechanics lien law, abolition of wage payments in script; direct popular election of Senators; taxing the income from bonds, stocks, and mortgages;

restricting or banning the use of convict labor in the production of goods.

A number of these reforms were enacted in New Jersey in 1851 under the administration of Governor George F. Fort. Imprisonment for debt, nominally abolished in 1842, was banned in the new State Constitution of 1844. The legislature exempted from seizure the first $200 of a debtor; removed the property qualification for holding public office; limited working hours to 10 in cotton, wool, silk, paper, glass, flax, iron and brass manufacturing, and the minimum age of employment to ten years. However, the limitations on hours and child labor were not enforced.

Most significant of the acts of the Reform legislature of 1851 was the adoption of a free public school law. While many parties claim credit for this, Frank T. De Vyver concluded that it was the middle class reformers, not trade unionists or workers, who deserve the major plaudits:

> The movement for free public schools in New Jersey does not appear to have been a workingman's movement though there is no doubt that both in Newark and in Trenton the Workingmen's parties supported it. . . . The conclusion must be that it was the reformers who led for free education for all. The workingmen of the state were undoubtedly back of the movement, but they represented only one section of the great movement for free universal education.*

The same was true elsewhere in the country. Thus, George R. Taylor observed that "it now appears that the leadership and much of the impetus [for tax supported schools] came not from urban workers but from the middle class." **

* Frank T. De Vyver, "The Organization of Labor in New Jersey Before 1860" (Unpublished doctoral dissertation, Princeton University, 1934), 329-330.

** G. R. Taylor, "Preface to Vols. V and VI," in J. R. Commons *et al.* (eds.), *A Documentary History of American Industrial Society* (New York, 1958), IX.

Among the leading figures in the Trenton reform group were Dr. Charles Skelton, physician, small businessman, and in his youth an apprentice shoemaker; Franklin S. Mill, newspaper owner and publisher, mayor and justice of the peace; Charles W. Jay, publisher, editor, city clerk, and one-time official in the Philadelphia Customs House. Skelton, by far the most popular reformist leader, was elected to Congress twice as a Democrat, serving from 1851 to 1855 in a seat that heretofore had been safely Whig.

UTOPIAN REFORM AND AGRARIANISM

After the depression of 1837 wiped out most of the unions and associations of unions, there was no resurgence of union organization accompanying the business revivals of 1843 and 1846. Instead of a renewal of union organization there was a pause, a period of new experimentation for labor, a turn toward utopian systems of social organization and land reform. These movements represent a distinct break with the previous history of labor.

Trade unions did exist, but their number was few. For example there was a Saddlers' and Harness Makers' Union in Newark which demanded and won a wage increase in 1844. A hatters' union, also in Newark, joined with hatters from New York and perhaps from other nearby states in an effort to get a uniform wage in the industry. Employers who acceded to these demands were declared "fair" while those which did not were labeled "foul." Newark had some of each. Shoemakers in Burlington were reported on strike in 1845; likewise shoemakers in Trenton struck in 1847 and 1848. In all three instances, demands for higher wages were responsible for the disputes.

Compared to the number of unions and strikes of the 1830's, however, the number from 1840 to 1850 was very small. Perhaps the sparseness of union organization may be attributed to the weakness of the unions in facing the depression of 1837, and the poor economic conditions and misery that characterized the decade of the 1840's. Until the gold discoveries in California in 1849 sparked a more pronounced prosperity, the decade was known as the "hungry forties." In Trenton, for example, there were continuing efforts by philanthropists, reformers, and workers to help the unemployed.

Instead of unions and strikes, the dominant theme of the period was a turn to alternatives to capitalism. But the philosophic point of view of the utopian and agrarian movements was reactionary and unreal. They favored a return to a fictional, historic past, or a social order that came from the drawing-board, and rejected the industrial revolution, capitalism, and an urban way of life. In essence, they rejected life as it was in favor of life as it might be. The principal movements were Association, Agrarianism, and Cooperation.

These movements were based on esoteric theorization and programs of social re-organization, and were chiefly the work of intellectuals rather than workers. Roughly from 1840 to the early 1850's, middle-class intellectuals dominated labor's philosophy and interests. Meanwhile, the organization of unions receded into the background. Because the intellectuals did dominate the labor scene in this period, and because of the failure of these movements to achieve significant results for labor, the union movement in this country has ever since been wary of intellectuals and their theorizations about the social order. It partly explains the conservative outlook of so many labor leaders and labor programs which came afterward.

The Associationists favored social arrangements that would enable men to express their natural bent toward cooperation rather than competition. It rejected the theory of class struggle. The outstanding example of associationist theory in practice was Charles Fourier's Phalanx, an ideal cooperative community which was to consist of from 1500 to 1600 persons living together in a single building. The members were not to be equal in status and income. The income of the phalanx was to be allocated five-twelfths to labor, four-twelfths to capital and three-twelfths for special talents. The economy was based on agriculture, with an admixture of private and common ownership. The idea originated in France and was brought to America by Albert Brisbane, father of the Hearst newspaperman, Arthur Brisbane. However, it was Horace Greeley who gave the idea an opportunity to be tried. During the 1840's more than forty communities were established, most of them failing in short order.

The most successful was the North American Phalanx established in September, 1843, near Freehold, New Jersey. Little more than a year later, it consisted of 77 members of whom 26 were children under sixteen; and its land was valued at $28,000. Eight years later, membership had risen to 112, and the property holdings to $80,000. However, a split developed in 1855, with the secessionists moving to Raritan Bay and forming a new phalanx there. Within two years the North American ended in failure: perhaps due to a fire that destroyed a mill and the crop, perhaps to further disagreement among the inhabitants.

The New Jersey Phalanx attracted many famous visitors. Horace Greeley often visited the North American Phalanx, reportedly being fond of "snoozing in a rocker on the porch of the phalanastery * (the apartment-like housing unit of a phalanx). In addition, Greeley became a vice-president of the community. Georges Clemenceau, later Prime Minister of France, came to see the Phalanx when he was a young doctor in New York. George Arnold, writer and poet died there; while Alexander Woollcott, noted critic, was born on the grounds of the North American Phalanx in 1887, the grandson of John Bucklin who had been a member. Most of the buildings of the Phalanx were destroyed by fire in 1854. Shortly afterward, in the winter of 1855-1856, the society disbanded.**

* *Asbury Park Press*, Oct. 18, 1964.
** Harold F. Wilson, "The North American Phalanx," in the *Proceedings* of The New Jersey Historical Society, LXX, 1952, 208.

Headquarters of North American Phalanx
Sketch by Vernon Howe Bailey
Courtesy of New Jersey Division, Newark Public Library

The second of the new schemes, Agrarianism, proposed to give public land free to those who would till it and set up rural townships. It had little appeal to labor in New Jersey. At a meeting in Newark in 1845 of the National Reform Association, an organization devoted to free public land, a total of 40 persons was reported present. No subsequent involvement of labor groups in Newark is known.

Likewise, a New Jersey association for free soil, organized in 1851, dropped out of sight by 1852. As De Vyver noted, such movements "do not form an important part of the history of labor in New Jersey."

On the other hand, Cooperation had a distinctly practical appeal to urban workers and unionists. Their problems were not going to be solved in the new communities of the wilderness, but Cooperation could take root in a city, and therefore was a possible alternative to capitalism.

Both producers and consumers cooperatives were attempted. Producers' cooperatives, it was thought, would overcome industrial strikes and warfare and eventually perhaps replace the private system of production. In New Jersey, coachmakers in Rahway set up a producers' cooperative in 1859, which may have lasted through the Civil War. However, like the Association schemes, the producers' cooperatives movement also failed. A variety of reasons accounted for its demise: inadequate and improper organization, lack of good management, competition from private enterprise, and the Civil War.

Similar factors contributed to the failure of consumers' cooperatives. In New Jersey, a consumers cooperative was established in Upper Rahway in 1852. Other cooperatives appeared in Trenton in 1854 and Jersey City in 1859, but these, too, did not survive the Civil War.

REVIVAL OF UNIONISM

Workers gradually turned away from utopianism and land reform, and under the encouragement of more favorable times actively began to organize unions in the decade of the 1850's. The issue which led to a definite break between union labor and the intellectual reformers was labor's demand for shorter hours with no reduction in pay. The reformists favored shorter hours, but with a proportionate reduction in pay. New Jersey's ten-hour law of 1851 left the issue unsettled, so when the law was applied in Paterson's textile mills, employers reduced workers' pay. A strike followed which was settled with a compromise.

Henry Vethake, in keeping with his strong belief in competition and laissez faire condemned laws regulating the hours of work as well as unions. Unlike the reformers, he was at least consistent in his views:

"Since laws reducing hours in effect raise wages, they too are vicious," he stated. Like union demands for wage increases, "they mean a fall in the rate of profits."

Even more alarming, however, Vethake foresaw a Malthusian rise in population following an increase in wages, but then a return to former levels as the increased labor supply depressed wages. Thus, unions and labor in New Jersey or the country could not escape Ricardo's iron law of wages. As Vethake put it:

The rise in wages will lead to the increase of population with unusual rapidity; while the fall in the rate of profits will lead to a less rapid accumulation of capital. Thus wages will fall gradually to their former rate and so closely approach it as to be no sufficient compensation to society for the violation of the rights of property implied in every compulsory raising of the wages rate.[*]

Labor attitudes and techniques underwent a marked change in the decade before the Civil War. Labor accepted capitalism, the workers' position in it as wage-earners, the inevitability of industrial disputes, and that workers ought to rely primarily on themselves to gain improvements in their living standards. It was a more

[*] Joseph Dorfman, *The Economic Mind in American Civilization* (New York, 1946), II, 737.

limited approach but one that was definite and possible of attainment.

Partly as a result of these changes, and because of improving business, there was a marked revival of unionism during the fifties. The continued growth of the cities between 1850 and 1860 sharply increased the demand for building tradesmen and led to the resurgence of unions among carpenters, masons, painters, laborers, and stone cutters in Newark, Trenton, Paterson, Jersey City, and Burlington. The building trades revived with the brightening of economic conditions in the late 1840's.

Women organized unions in ladies' hat manufacturing in Newark. One, the Milliners Union, was established in 1850; another, the Hat Trimmers, in 1859. Some dressmakers were organized, too. The girls were reported as "obliged to labor at least eleven hours per day, and on Saturday usually sixteen hours." In trying to reduce their hours in 1850, the Milliners appealed to the "Ladies of Newark and the influence of gentlemen" to help them, but with no success.

Male hatters organized in Orange and struck twice in 1854 and 1857 over wages. A shoemakers' society in Newark struck in 1850 and again in 1852. Both strikes were over wages, the first to resist a wage cut and the second to gain a wage increase.

The movement toward national organization in a trade was responsible for setting up a number of local unions in New Jersey. Thus a printers local made its first appearace in New Jersey when printers in Trenton organized under the impetus of the national union of printers. Similarly, a local union was formed among printers in 1857 in Newark and another in Jersey City in 1860.

The founding of the National Molders Union in 1859 contributed to the re-appearance of local unions in this trade in Paterson in 1859, and in Jersey City in 1860.

After the Civil War, the *national* impetus to local organization became more important. Hence, in order to understand the local scene the orientation of labor history begins to shift more toward national developments.

The forerunners of the modern union movement in New Jersey did not take root so soon as precursors in other states did, notably those in Pennsylvania and New York. This was largely due, it appears, to the lag of urbanization in the State. In the early 1830's, however, a vigorous local union movement arose in Newark and other towns primarily among skilled workers in leather manufacturing and building.

In contrast, in cotton manufacturing, where the industrial revolution started, no unions were established although there was a number of strikes reflecting the poor working conditions in the mills.

The promising union movement among skilled workers of the thirties disappeared under the depression of 1837, and no important revival in organization took place until the 1850's. In that decade, a significant new form of labor organization appeared on the scene: the national union. Thereafter it became a factor which increasingly affected the development of local unions.

III

LABOR FEDERATIONS
1860-1890

THE MODERN UNION MOVEMENT in New Jersey and the Nation was not established until the end of the nineteenth century when two labor federations were organized: the New Jersey State Labor Congress in 1879, and the American Federation of Labor in 1886. In 1883, the State Labor Congress became the Federation of Trades and Labor Unions of New Jersey, and this organization affiliated with the American Federation of Labor about 1888.

Unionism's break-through in New Jersey as in the Nation was limited to skilled workers in the industries in which technology lagged, while it left unorganized the unskilled in the industries in which technology was advancing most rapidly. Selig Perlman described affiliates of the American Federation of Labor as existing "in well-defined trades which were not affected by technical changes." *

Basically, the cause retarding a permanent union movement in both New Jersey and the country were the rapid growth of the economy, the workers' ability to move up in the social order, and the recurrent tides of immigration.

For New Jersey unionists, the competition of foreign

* Selig Perlman, "Upheaval and Reorganization," in J. R. Commons *et al.* (eds.), *History of Labour in the United States* (New York, 1918), II, 320.

labor often meant loss of jobs and strikes. Thus, the vice-president of the Freight Handlers' Union of Jersey City, in the last days of their strike in 1883 or 1884, when the tide had turned against them and hope was gone, exclaimed, "It's that—Castle Garden [an immigration center in New York City] that's killing us."

When forced to admit that the work he and his brethren claimed as their specialty could be done and well done by Italians and Hungarians, just a faint conception of the source from which the strongest competition with his labor was coming dawned upon him, and he like the dweller upon the Sand Lots of San Francisco, was ready to take up the cry: "We are ruined by foreign cheap labor." *

Public policy, still primarily in the hands of the courts, was opposed to limitations on a free market for labor and therefore was usually against unions. Employer opposition, too, played an important role in retarding unionism's advance, but it would not have been nearly so successful were not the technological and economic factors already such formidable barriers.

While all national forces affecting labor from 1860 to 1890 influenced the course of unionism in New Jersey as well, the first national association of labor organizations to make a decisive impression in the state were the Knights of Labor. The Knights did not come into New Jersey until 1874, so we must briefly note those developments which, between 1860 and 1874, loomed most important on the national scene, and which also affected local events.

The first of these was the Civil War. Initially, the War hurt unionism. Southern unions were separated from northern unions (some being locals of national organizations), while hostilities at first caused a slowdown in business and employment and a drop in union organization. However, the government's policy of paying for part of its war needs through borrowing and

* New Jersey Bureau of Statistics of Labor and Industries, *Seventh Annual Report, 1884*, 295.

successive issues of greenbacks quickly turned recession into prosperity and fostered the revival and formation of unions. Thus, between December, 1863, and December, 1864, the total number of unions increased from 79 to 270 for the country as a whole (the South excluded). According to an authoritative history of American labor, the number of unions in New Jersey increased only from 4 to 10 in this period.* However, scattered evidence from the *Newark Daily Advertiser* indicates that the increase was much greater.

Another national force which affected the course of unionism was the nation-wide extension of markets for goods and labor by the railway system. Railway mileage grew from just over 8000 miles in 1850 to nearly 31,000 miles by 1860, to 35,000 by the end of the Civil War, and 53,000 miles by 1870. The East-West link was completed on the first transcontinental railway in May, 1869. Railway mileage in New Jersey doubled between 1850 and 1860, and doubled again in the following decade.

These forces—the Civil War and the nation-wide extension of markets—stimulated the development of nation-wide forms of labor organization. In little over a year, 1864-1865, ten new national unions were formed, compared to five in the eight years between 1852 and 1860. Among the new nationals were such now familiar organizations as the Cigar Makers, the Plasterers, the Bricklayers and Masons, and the Painters.

One national union formed in 1859 which had a number of local affiliates in New Jersey was the Iron Molders union.** This union organized workers in stove manufacture and hollow-ware. A local molders union from Jersey City participated in the founding of the national in Philadelphia, July 4, 1859. A leading figure

* John B. Andrews, "Nationalisation," in J. R. Commons *et al.*, *History of Labour in the United States* (New York, 1918), 19.
** Jonathan Grossman, *William Sylvis, Pioneer of American Labor* (New York, 1945).

in the national union came from that Jersey City local, Isaac J. Neall. Neall was president of the national in 1860-1861 and continued to play an active role in the union afterward. He was an associate of William Sylvis, the Iron Molders' most prominent leader and one of the earliest labor leaders to gain nation-wide recognition.

During the Civil War there were local unions of the Iron Molders in Paterson, Newark, and Elizabethport as well as Jersey City. The local in Elizabethport struck in 1864, but without conforming to the rules of the national union. As a result, Sylvis urged a return to work, thus ending the strike.

The New Jersey locals like most other molders' locals were wiped out in the wake of the depression after the Civil War, which touched bottom in 1868.

Between 1865 and 1873, about 18 national unions were set up, but how many locals in New Jersey joined or were organized by the nationals in this period is unknown. One local, Newark Typographical Local 103, which was formed in 1867 as part of a national union, still exists. It may well be the oldest, continuously functioning union in the State. With the collapse of so many national unions in the years 1873-1877 (a period of long and severe depression) most locals in New Jersey no doubt also disappeared.

In South Jersey, the New Jersey Bureau of Statistics of Labor and Industry reported in 1878 that "the Hollow Ware Glassblowers are the only numerous body of workingmen in the district that have steadily maintained a trade organization during the past fifteen years." *

ATTEMPTS AT NATIONAL FEDERATION

The first national association of unions since the National Trades Union of 1834-1837 was organized in 1864. It was the International Industrial Assembly of

* New Jersey Bureau of Statistics of Labor and Industry, *First Annual Report, 1878,* 117-118.

North America. However, the Assembly's initial meeting was also its last. For unknown reasons no organizations from New Jersey attended the meeting held in Louisville, Kentucky.

After the Civil War, in 1866, another nation-wide association of unions was organized, the National Labor Union. Among individuals from New Jersey whose activities led to its formation were Isaac J. Neall, from the molders union in Jersey City, N. H. Crane of the curriers in Newark, and John Reed of the carpenters in Jersey City. Within a short time after its founding, the purely labor programs and policies of the National Labor Union became secondary to those of farmers and political reformers. Instead of being an association of unions, as its name might suggest, the National Labor Union became "a typical American politico-reform organization led by labor leaders without organizations, politicians without parties, women without husbands, and cranks, visionaries, and agitators without jobs." *

Eventually, the National Labor Union formed a labor party, the National Labor and Reform Party, but the party was stillborn, since its presidential candidate for the election of 1872, Judge David Davis of Illinois, withdrew. The Party's vice-presidential choice was Governor Joel Parker of New Jersey.

The demise of the National Labor Union and its political offspring was soon followed by a fresh attempt at a national association, the Industrial Congress. The Congress was organized just two months before the financial panic of 1873, by a group of national unions, the Iron Molders, the Machinists and Blacksmiths, the Coopers, and the Typographical Union, and what might have been a promising beginning was choked off by the panic; the Congress, later re-named the Industrial Brotherhood, hung on until 1878. In New Jersey, branches of the Industrial Brotherhood joined a national movement

* Norman Ware, *The Labor Movement in the United States, 1860-1895* (New York, 1964), 11.

in consumer cooperation, the Sovereigns of Industry, but this group, too, was short lived, passing out of existence in 1878.

The disintegration of the union movement continued under the impact of the long depression of the 1870's, and did not revive until business activity improved in 1878. Initially, the trades assembly or council (an association of local unions in a city or county) showed the quickest response to the improvement in economic conditions. These performed on the economic, legislative, and political levels giving affiliated unions the same type of support as nationals gave their locals. They often served a mediatory role between an affiliated local and an employer, a function less suited to a national. They also became leaders in the use of the boycott.

In New Jersey, several such local assemblies appear. One of the first was the Newark Trades Assembly of 1879. Eight or nine organizations founded the Assembly. Initially it was not very active, but between 1882 and 1886 it showed more vigor in advocating the abolition of convict labor to produce goods sold in competition with that produced by free workers.

The most important assembly, the Essex Trade Assembly, was organized in 1880. Like the Newark Trades Assembly, it was also originated by the Knights of Labor, whose activities in New Jersey will be sketched hereafter. Unions as well as local assemblies of the Knights were affiliated.

A Trades Assembly in Hudson County was set up in May, 1885. The roster of officers suggests that this assembly was made up more of trade union than Knights of Labor members. Among the officers were a machinist, an ironworker, an iron molder, and a stationary engineer, trades which were usually organized by unions rather than by the Knights.

National unions also revived under the more congenial economic climate after 1878. Locally, this meant the formation of new unions belonging to a national union, a process which began slowly in 1878 and thereafter picked up considerable momentum through most of the 1880's. (See Table 3.) By 1881, the revival of labor organization led to yet another attempt at association, the Federation of Organized Trades and Labor Unions of the United States and Canada. Initially comprising Knights of Labor and trade unionists, the organization gradually became an association of trade unions. However it was a weak organization and upon its dissolution was succeeded by the American Federation of Labor in 1886.

The establishment of the modern union movement in the form of the American Federation of Labor was not accomplished, however, without a sharp challenge from a rival labor organization, the Knights of Labor. The Knights preceded both the American Federation of Labor and the Federation of Organized Trades and Labor Unions of the United States and Canada, and was the first national association of labor to make its influence felt in New Jersey.

The organizer of the Knights was a native of New Jersey, Uriah S. Stephens. Stephens was born in Cape May in 1821. He was trained for the Baptist ministry, taught school for a time, but earned his living as a tailor. It is claimed that Stephens had traveled to Europe and had been exposed to Marxist thought, but if he had been, neither he nor the Knights showed evidence of Marxist influence. As a brief examination will show, the Knights' program and actions shared little with Communist thought and tactics.

Stephens organized the first unit of the Knights among his fellow garment workers, six in number, in Philadelphia at the end of 1869. The unit was named a local assembly. As the Knights grew, many other local assemblies were also organized on an occupational basis, exactly like the locals of trade unions. However, still other locals combined workers of diverse occupations.

Membership in the Knights was opened to all who worked or had worked for a living except lawyers, doctors, bankers, purveyors of liquor, stockbrokers, and professional gamblers. Thus, the Knights became an organization embracing *all classes of labor,* unskilled and skilled alike. In this it differed radically from the trade unions who were made up almost exclusively of skilled workers.

The program of the Knights rejected the class struggle and with it conflict between workers and capitalists. The Knights, at least its leadership, consequently opposed the strike. Their ultimate solution for labor was the establishment of cooperative production and consumption, and thus a cooperative commonwealth. As Terence V. Powderly, successor to Stephens as Grand Master Workman (President) of the national organization of the Knights put it, "My belief that cooperation shall one day take the place of the wage system remains unshaken." *

Initially, the Knights made little headway in organizing, but with the depression of 1873, many unattached locals and locals of disintegrating national unions turned to the Knights for refuge in a storm. By the end of 1873 more than 80 locals located in or near the large eastern cities, Philadelphia, New York, Trenton, Wilmington, and Boston, had joined the Knights of Labor.

Despite its aversion to strikes, the Knights did become involved in and won important strikes in 1883-1884 and again in 1885. These successes attracted thousands to the organization. From a membership of just over 28,000 in 1880, the Knights increased their following to nearly 180,000 in 1883, and to over 700,000 by 1886. So large were the Knights in that year that they dwarfed the newly-born American Federation of Labor whose total membership was a mere 138,000.**

But defeat was mixed with the victories as workers became overconfident of the power of the Knights. They

* Quoted from Terence V. Powderly, *The Path I Trod,* in Foster R. Dulles, *Labor in America* (New York, 1963), 137.
** Leo Wolman, *The Growth of American Trade Unions 1880-1923* (New York, 1924), Table 1, 32.

turned too freely to strikes, and then most of them ended in defeat, with great losses of membership for the Knights of Labor.

In 1886, while still at their peak, the Knights challenged the AFL for supremacy in the labor movement. It was a clash between a giant labor organization dedicated to the principle of the solidarity of all labor, unskilled as well as skilled, and a small group limiting their interests and goals to the skilled. It would not be a great exaggeration to contrast the two as the "labor masses" (the Knights) versus the "labor aristocrats" (the AFL).

Despite the great size of the Knights in 1886, the contest was a David and Goliath affair, ending in the defeat of the Knights and its ultimate downfall. The Knights turned increasingly to politics and were finally captured by agrarian reformers in 1893. By that year, its number had dwindled to about 75,000; the AFL counted some 260,000 members in 1893. In this way ended the clash between an organization based on craft, represented by the AFL, and an organization for all workers, including the unskilled, represented by the Knights.

THE KNIGHTS IN NEW JERSEY

The impact of the Knights of Labor in New Jersey was threefold: First, it stimulated the formation of many local organizations, giving the State a period of active organization the like of which had not been seen since the early 1830's.

Second, the Knights originated the labor association which became the New Jersey State Federation of Labor, AFL. (This organization retained its identity until becoming the State AFL-CIO in 1961.)

Finally, the Knights also founded other labor groups which have continued to this day. Among these was the Essex County Trades Assembly, the predecessor of the present Essex County Trades Council, the leading county association of unions in New Jersey.

The Knights first appeared in New Jersey at the end

of 1873 or the beginning of 1874. The first local assembly, one of stone cutters, was set up in Trenton either in December, 1873, or January, 1874. The local assembly traced its origins to a union which claimed to date back to 1833. It was followed by another, Local Assembly 31, consisting of ship caulkers in Camden. Other locals were soon established so that by the fall of 1874, a District Assembly was set up in Camden. However, it was more an extension of the Philadelphia District Assembly than a separate organization, and had vanished as an operating unit of the Knights by 1878. Window glass workers in South Jersey became part of Local Assembly 300, a national union.

Until 1885, the growth of the Knights was slow in New Jersey. In 1886, its biggest year, over one hundred assemblies joined the Knights. The New Jersey peak corresponded to the Knights' peak nationally. In 1887, the total number of organizations within the New Jersey Knights was over 240 (Table 1), but this number was below the peak of the year before.

TABLE 1

NUMBER OF LOCAL ASSEMBLIES 1874-1887 *

Year	Number	Year	Number
1874 **	3	1881	3
1875	1	1882	3
1876	1	1883	5
1877	9	1884	4
1878	1	1885	58
1879	6	1886	122
1880	1	1887	24
	Total		241

* New Jersey Bureau of Statistics of Labor and Industry, *Tenth Annual Report, 1887*, 17.

** The Bureau reports these as organized in 1873. Norman Ware, in *The Labor Movement in the United States, 1860-1890* (New York, 1964), 30, dates these organizations as of December, 1873, or January, 1874, and inclines to the later year. We have followed his chronology.

Nevertheless the Knights of Labor in New Jersey in 1887 greatly outnumbreed the trades unions both in the number of organizations and in membership. Thus, their total claimed state membership in 231 assemblies was over 40,000 (Table 2). Compared to this the trades unions, which did not belong to the Knights, claimed

TABLE 2

MEMBERSHIP, KNIGHTS OF LABOR, BY INDUSTRY, 1887 *

	Number of Assemblies	Per Cent of Total	Membership	Per Cent of Total
MANUFACTURING	**140**	**59.1**	**24,658**	**61.2**
Food, Drink, Tobacco	11	4.6	867	2.2
Apparel	10	4.2	1,914	4.7
Transportation Equipment	4	1.7	721	1.8
Chemical, glass, rubber, clay, and stone products	27	11.4	3,840	9.5
Lumber and wood products	1	.5	50	.1
Textiles	27	11.4	6,598	16.4
Printing and Engraving	1	.5	37	.1
Leather and shoes	15	6.3	2,907	7.2
Machinery and metal products	38	16.0	6,750	16.8
Paper and paper products	2	.8	69	.2
Misc. manufacturing	4	1.7	905	2.2
NON-MANUFACTURING	**39**	**16.4**	**4,162**	**10.4**
Building	14	5.9	1,536	3.8
Transportation	18	7.6	2,005	5.0
(Railways)**	(9)	(3.8)	(996)	(2.5)
Services	4	1.7	464	1.2
Retail and wholesale trade	3	1.2	157	.4
NOT CLASSIFIED	**58**	**24.5**	**11,455**	**28.4**
Totals	237 †	100.0	40,275	100.0

* New Jersey Bureau of Statistics of Labor and Industry, *Tenth Annual Report, 1887,* 28 and 30.
** Included in transportation.
† Excludes four assemblies not reporting membership.

about 18,000 members in some 158 organizations in New Jersey.

Significantly, the Knights' strength centered in manufacturing industries and embraced both skilled and unskilled workers. In this respect it was much like the industrial composition of the unions of the Congress of Industrial Organizations in our own times.

Women made up nearly 11 per cent of the Knights' membership, compared to a much lower figure, about 3 per cent, for the trade unions, reflecting the Knights' greater concern for and success in organizing the unskilled worker.

The number of trade unions functioning in New Jersey in 1887 was far fewer than local assemblies of the Knights. Information covering 126 of the 158 unions reported in 1887 was available for the purpose of dating the year of their formation (Table 3).

The oldest known union as of 1887 was an organization of Brown Stone Cutters in Newark. It was not affiliated with any national union and claimed 400 members. Of the total number of unions functioning in 1887, 113 were affiliated with a national union and 45 were local independents.

Table 3 indicates that the union movement was mainly formed in the 1880's. Of the 126 unions reported in the table, 98 were organized in the period 1880-1887. Defunct unions are not recorded in the table and therefore the activity of New Jersey workers in forming unions was doubtless greater than the table shows. Nevertheless, it does indicate that the union movement in New Jersey moved with national trends.

In contrast to the Knights, the strength of the trade unions was concentrated in skilled workers in non-manufacturing industries, principally building, followed by railway transportation (Table 4).

The manufacturing industries which had some trade union representation were apparel (particularly hat-making), clay, glass, and stone.

Geographically, the preponderance of trade union

TABLE 3

Number of Trades Unions 1834-1887 *

Year	Number	Year	Number
1834	1	1878	2
1849	2	1879	6
1854	3	1880	5
1857	4	1881	10
1862	3	1882	4
1864	1	1883	3
1865	1	1884	12
1867	2	1885	18
1868	2	1886	24
1870	1	1887	22
		Total	126

membership in 1887 like that of the Knights was in northern New Jersey. Essex County led in membership with most of its members concentrated in Newark. Then came Hudson, followed by Passaic in third place. The three counties together accounted for nearly 90 per cent of the total.

Trade union apprenticeship practices in skilled occupations that now characterize craft unions were already widely regulated by New Jersey unions in 1887. Some 59 unions representing 19 trade occupations reported regulation of apprentices, as did 27 local assemblies of the Knights.

With respect to benefit features, 93 unions and 20 local assemblies provided these. Typical benefit payments made by unions in New Jersey are shown in Table 5. Annual dues for unionists ranged from $1.20 to $19.20; the Knights' dues averaged about $3.00 a year.** The lower dues charged by the Knights indicates that they organized lower-paid workers, and that they could not

* New Jersey, Bureau of Statistics of Labor and Industry, *Tenth Annual Report, 1887*, 17.

** New Jersey Bureau of Statistics of Labor and Industry, *Tenth Annual Report, 1887*.

TABLE 4

MEMBERSHIP OF TRADE UNIONS BY INDUSTRY, 1887 *
UNIONS FORMED ANUALLY IN NEW JERSEY *

	Number of Unions	Per Cent of Total	Membership	Per Cent of Total
MANUFACTURING	68	43.0	8,067	45.3
Food, Drink, Tobacco	11	6.9	1,192	6.7
Apparel	18	11.4	4,254	23.9
Transportation Equipment	2	1.3	188	1.1
Chemical, clay, rubber glass, stone products	23	14.6	1,336	7.5
Textiles	—		—	
Lumber and wood products	1	.6	105	.6
Printing and engraving	5	3.2	388	2.2
Leather and shoes	1	.6	55	.3
Machinery and metal products	5	3.2	374	2.1
Paper and paper products	1	.6	150	.8
Misc. manufacturing	1	.6	25	.1
NON-MANUFACTURING	90	57.0	9,723	54.7
Building **	55	34.8	6,710	37.7
Transportation	30	19.0	2,411	13.6
(Railways) †	(28)	(17.7)	(2,096)	(11.8)
Services	3	1.9	436	2.5
Retail and wholesale trade	2	1.3	166	.9
Totals	158	100.0	17,790	100.0

as a rule finance benefit programs like those of the higher-paid, skilled trade unionists. To get unemployment, sickness, retirement or other benefits, the low-paid, unskilled workers would have to turn to the government. And in fact, this is what happened. The Knights and later groups who championed the "labor

* New Jersey Bureau of Statistics of Labor and Industry, *Tenth Annual Report, 1887*, 24 and 26.
** Adjusted to include two Associations in Monmouth County not included in the original table.
† Included in transportation.

TABLE 5

BENEFIT PROGRAMS OF TRADES UNIONS, 1887 *

Weekly Allocation for:

Union	Annual Per Capita	Unemployment	Sickness	Retirement
Engineers	$15.58	$7.89	$2.84	$3.17
Carpenters and Joiners	14.07	7.93	3.41	.61
Steam Engine Makers	10.90	5.57	2.60	1.45
Bricklayers	6.95	—	3.56	.08
Compositors (London)	7.70	4.02	—	—
Bookbinders	9.82	6.64	2.31	.31
Blacksmiths	8.65	6.81	2.48	.46
Cabinet Makers	13.94	8.76	1.58	—
Cotton Spinners	15.26	4.50	—	.23
Railway Workers	4.70	.28	.09	—

masses" continuously sought to improve the material lot of the unskilled through protective labor legislation and public programs of social security.

THE STATE LABOR CONGRESS AND FEDERATION

The most important result of the Knights' activities in New Jersey was the founding of the State Labor Congress in 1879. A successor organization affiliated itself with the AFL about nine years later, in 1888. Thus, contrary to the currently accepted version of the origin of the New Jersey State Federation of Labor, AFL, the Congress was a product of the Knights of Labor, not the trade unions. Consequently, this invalidates the claim of the State AFL to date its beginnings from 1879, seven years before the founding of the American Federation of Labor.

The evidence for our conclusion is found in the career of the founder of the State Labor Congress, John

* New Jersey Bureau of Statistics of Labor and Industry, *Tenth Annual Report, 1887,* 150.

W. Hayes, the founding of the Congress, the identity of the founding labor organizations, the tactics of the Congress, its program, and the history of the Congress and the State Federation.

To begin with, Hayes, the founder of the State Labor Congress, was one of the leading figures in the Knights of Labor, and, in fact, was its last Grand Master Workman, from 1902 to 1917. Before that he had been the secretary-treasurer of the Knights, and editor of its journal, the *National Labor Digest*. He enjoyed a long and intimate friendship with Terence V. Powderly, probably the best known of the Grand Master Workmen, and leader of the Knights at its peak. Hayes broke with Powderly and contributed to his defeat in the presidential election of the Knights in 1893. So important was Hayes in the Knights that "it was only when his [Powderly's] closest friend and associate, John W. Hayes, turned against him in 1893 that the combined socialist and farmer faction got him out." *

Hayes was a member of the Railroad Telegraphers Union, one of the two national trade unions to belong to the Knights as a national trade district. He became a telegrapher to earn a living after he lost his right arm as brakeman on the Pennsylvania Railroad. It seems reasonable to infer that Hayes was one of the reasons the Railroad Telegraphers belonged to the Knights.

At this time (in the late 1870's and early 1880's), Hayes, like many of his contemporaries, could belong both to the Knights and a trade union without any conflict of loyalty. It was not until the struggle between the Knights and the AFL broke out in the later part of the 1880's that dual membership clearly became a violation of trade union principles. Then workers had to choose between the narrow principle of exclusive jurisdiction, the bedrock of the AFL, and the general principle of "labor solidarity" of the Knights.

* Norman J. Ware, *The Labor Movement in the United States, 1860-1895* (New York, 1964), 103.

Hayes' relations with the trade unionists was amicable until the struggle between the Knights and the AFL broke out in 1886. At that time Hayes stood with the Knights and described the unions as selfish sectarians who ignored the masses of workers.*

In 1929, in an address to the Convention of the New Jersey State Federation of Labor, AFL, Hayes recounted the origin and purposes of founding the State Labor Congress. By the end of the 1870's, he pointed out, there were no important union groups either nationally or in the state. Furthermore, he said:

The great mass of the people, men and women who toiled in the various crafts, callings and grades of employment were not, at that time and for many years thereafter, considered fitting material, by the leaders of the unions, in that day and generation as being worthy or even competent for organization, and women particularly were denied the right to organize for their own protection. The result being that while the unions were unable to cover with their so-called shield of protection the members in their own trade, yet the toilers in all the multifarious branches of labor, who were never dignified with the name of "Trade Worker" were denied the right to organize for their own protection, but were privileged to walk the streets during strikes and lock-outs, suffering for the necessaries of life on account of labor troubles which they had no voice in creating.**

The Knights of Labor, however, reached "out for every class of worker" and was composed of "tradesmen, mixed trades, women in factories and other establishments."

The Knights conducted their organizing in secret, Hayes explained, until 1878 when they began to abandon secrecy. In doing so, the Knights decided:

* Norman J. Ware, *The Labor Movement in the United States, 1860-1895* (New York, 1964), 276.

** John W. Hayes, *Address* to the Annual Convention of the New Jersey State Federation of Labor, 1929. Files of I. Kerrison, Special Mss. Collections, New Jersey Room, Rutgers University Library.

all Local Assemblies should adopt and use an outside name of some kind by which they could rent halls, hold public meetings and do all kinds of outside business without bringing the name of the Order or its members, as such, into public notice. Then it was that the first convention of the New Jersey Labor Congress was called to meet here in the City of New Brunswick in the Fall of 1879, fifty years ago.*

If we were to examine the background of the delegations to the first meeting of the State Labor Congress held in New Brunswick in 1879, we find that the largest representation came from local assemblies of the Knights. There were 14 local assemblies from the Knights, 4 different unions of hatters, 3 potters' unions, and one each of glass bottle blowers, printers, and shoemakers. John W. Hayes, was chosen as the first chairman or president of the Congress, and Charles H. Simmerman, a Knight and member of the glass workers as secretary. Through the influence of Hayes and the Congress (Knights of Labor), Simmerman became Secretary of the State Bureau of Statistics of Labor and Industries. He later became chief of that Bureau.

The over-riding purpose of the State Labor Congress was the abolition of the use of convict labor in competition with free workers, a policy of greatest concern to the unskilled and therefore of central importance to the Knights of Labor. In addition, the Congress worked for the elimination of the payment of wages in company script redeemable only at the company store, and the use of child labor.** While these were also objectives of the trade unions, the primary beneficiaries were the mass of unskilled workers, about whom the Knights were more concerned than the trade unionists.

In describing the methods of the State Labor Congress,

* John W. Hayes, *Address* to the Annual Convention of the New Jersey State Federation of Labor, 1929. Files of I. Kerrison, Special Mss. Collections, New Jersey Room, Rutgers University Library.
** New Jersey Bureau of Statistics of Labor and Industry, *Tenth Annual Report, 1887,* 98.

Hayes declared that "it fell to our lot to spread the light, to show the necessity for organization among *all classes of workers* and to lay the groundwork for a healthy public opinion upon the subject of labor." *

These remarks reveal that the objects of the Congress were the same as the Knights': "spreading the light," the missionary concept, to "all classes of workers," unskilled as well as skilled, and reliance on the help of public opinion to gain the objectives of labor.

In order to win the support of the public, Hayes' proposed a typical Knights of Labor technique; he called on the organizations of the Congress

to appoint a publicity committee consisting of three of the most intelligent members whose duty, among other things, was to wait upon the ministers of all religious denominations and urge them . . . to set the first Sunday in January, 1880, on which to preach a sermon on the subject of labor and its relations to the welfare of the State.**

The second meeting of the State Labor Congress was held a year later in Newark when some fifty delegates from all counties but Warren and Sussex appeared. Apparently, the Congress was fairly successful in gaining support and interest as evidenced by the large increase in the number of delegations. The secretary of the first Congress, Charles H. Simmerman, succeeded Hayes as president.

The Congress had become so prominent that by 1883 there was a movement to form a more permanent organization. Hitherto the Congress was merely an annual convention of workingmen's organizations; now the

* John W. Hayes, *Address* to the Annual Convention of the New Jersey State Federation of Labor, 1929. Files of I. Kerrison, Special Mss. Collections, New Jersey Room, Rutgers University Library.

** John W. Hayes, *Address* to the Annual Convention of the New Jersey State Federation of Labor, 1929. Files of I. Kerrison, Special Mss. Collections, New Jersey Room, Rutgers University Library.

majority of delegates wanted a central body with enlarged powers. As one delegate, an ex-Socialist and one-time Knight, Joseph Patrick McDonnell of Paterson put it, the majority assembled wanted a "federation in fact as well as name." By means of "the central head," he argued, "the various organizations of the state should be in constant communications with each other, an earnest propaganda carried on, and sufficient funds raised for legislative and organizational purposes." *

There were 65 to 70 delegates who met at Polk's Hall in Trenton for the Congress' meeting in 1883. All labor organizations in the state were invited to attend the one-day session. The invitation was signed by the President of the State Labor Congress, M. E. Frost of Newark, and J. H. Saunderson, Secretary, both members of the Knights of Labor. John W. Hayes served as chairman of the credentials committee.

The delegates adopted a formal constitution and named the new organization the Federation of Trades and Labor Unions of New Jersey (Appendix B), the same name as that adopted by the aforementioned national grouping of labor organizations in 1881. While the national Federation of Organized Trades and Labor Unions became identified with a craft unionist point of view, at its founding in 1881, it, too, was made up of Knights and craft unionists. The New Jersey group was not affiliated with the national Federation.

The New Jersey Federation tried to balance the interests of the crafts and the unskilled. Its statement of purposes included the organization of both skilled and unskilled workers, demanded legislation favorable to the *wage-working classes* (emphasis supplied), and urged the formation of local trade (craft) or labor (unskilled workers) councils, and national and international trades and labor union alliances.

John W. Hayes was chosen president; William M. Mankes of Manville, vice-president; Goldsmith P. Hall

* Files of I. Kerrison, Special Mss. Collections, New Jersey Room, Rutgers University Library.

of Bridgeton, assistant secretary; and John Brindley of Trenton, treasurer. All were members of the Knights of Labor. G. Hall became a deputy inspector under the state's factory inspection law. Apropos of labor leaders going into political jobs, Local Assembly 1785 of the Knights of Labor from New Brunswick offered a resolution at the convention that officers of the State's Bureau of Factory and Workshop Inspection be nominated by the Federation.

Joseph P. McDonnell of Paterson was chosen chairman of the seven-member legislative committee, a post he held for many years thereafter. In the subsequent struggle between the Knights and the trade unionists, McDonnell became a supporter of the union viewpoint, and after the latter's victory continued in his post. His long service, from 1883 to 1897, as member and chairman of the legislative (later the executive) committee made him the best known of the Federation's top officers. He, rather than the president, made annual convention reports on the Federation's legislative, political, and organization activities. After the defeat of the Knights and until his retirement from office in 1897, his reports became increasingly comprehensive and a major feature of the annual convention.

But although he gave continuity to the legislative and political activities of the Federation during the closing years of the nineteenth century, he never dominated the Federation, nor did the Federation ever become a reflection of his kaleidoscopic ideas.

During the convention, the delegates were addressed by Lawrence T. Fell, Chief Factory Inspector, whose principal duty was to enforce the state's child labor law. Significantly, the inspectorship was the result of political pressure exerted by the Federation to get enforcement of the revised Child Labor Law of 1883.

Despite that law, Fell declared that children were still "shamefully treated," one reason being the connivance of parents to evade it. Fell promised that if he were given more assistance, he "would drag these destroyers of childhood from their self-imposed idleness and force them to contribute to the support and education of their little ones." *

By the second meeting of the Federation, (1884), disputes between Knights and the trade unionists had broken out. The credentials of a Knights' delegation were challenged, but probably accepted. Amity between the two groups was restored by a number of actions. Cigarmakers local 138 of Newark proposed that the Federation adopt a resolution recognizing both the white label of the Knights' cigarmakers, and the blue label of the trades unions. Labels showed that the cigars were made under good working conditions and therefore the only ones which organized workers should buy. The convention also endorsed Terence V. Powderly, Grand Master Workman (President) of the Knights, for the post of Commissioner of the United States Bureau of Statistics.

A Cigarmakers local from Paterson proposed that the New Jersey Federation send a delegate to the next convention of the Federation of Organized Trades and Labor Unions of the United States and Canada. There is no evidence, however, that the New Jersey Federation was affiliated with the national group.

Hayes was re-elected president, but did not serve out his term. D. C. Hapenny, vice president and member of local assembly 1378 (of the Knights), succeeded him. He probably was reelected in 1885, since it was Hapenny who officially called to order the Convention of 1886.

The incipient struggle between the Knights and the unionists in New Jersey came to a head in the Federation's Convention of 1886. Three candidates ran for the presidency: Dennis Mullins of Jersey City, member of District Assembly 49, Knights of Labor; Max Guter, a member of the Cigar Makers Union of Newark; and Henry D. Stokes, a member of the Hat Finishers Union of Orange. By 1886 it will be remembered, the national contest between the Knights and the AFL was underway, and the spearhead of the AFL's attack on the Knights

* *Proceedings of the Federation of Trades and Labor Unions of New Jersey, 1883,* 11.

was the Cigarmakers Union. On the other hand, District Assembly 49 of the Knights was noted for its anti-trade-union approach. Hence, the 1886 convention opened with the sides drawn up for a fight.

After a spirited contest, Mullins of the Knights won election to the presidency. Later in the proceedings, when a delegate moved a resolution aimed at some trade union adherents, possibly J. P. McDonnell, who had become a believer in the craft union approach, another fight broke out between the trade unionists and the Knights.

The resolution would require any candidate for membership on the Federation's legislative committee to pledge not to accept any state office under a law already in force or to be enacted during their term on the committee. McDonnell may have been the target since he was chairman of the legislative committee and three years later was specifically attacked because he was proposed by the committee for the post of Secretary of the New Jersey Bureau of Statistics of Labor and Industries.

But whoever was the target, Max Guter, the unsuccessful candidate for the presidency, objected to the resolution and protested "gag rule" when the chair (Mullins) gaveled through voice approval of the resolution.

A member of the Patrons of Husbandry, Grange No. 9, a farm movement, was chosen vice-president, again indicating the control of the Knights over the convention. Unlike the unionists, the Knights believed in the solidarity of all producers—farmers as well as workers. In his address to the Convention, the vice-president, Walter Pancoast of Salem, expressed his desire for closer cooperation between labor and the farmer. During pre-election maneuvering, Goldsmith P. Hall, former secretary and vice-president of the Congress, and then Deputy Factory Inspector for South Jersey played an important role in getting Pancoast elected.

Henry Stokes, the other unsuccessful candidate for president was chosen treasurer, and C. K. Barnhardt, a printer and member of the Knights from Trenton, was made secretary. Since Stokes was a trade unionist, his election to office suggests an effort by the Knights to conciliate the craft unionists in the Federation.

The program adopted by the Convention of 1886 showed the influence of the Knights, although it was one which trade unionists could accept. The convention called for equal taxation of all property (corporate or individual), compulsory education, working people to vote for their friends, government monopoly of note issue, and a more effective factory inspection law.

Mullins was returned to office in 1887, but declined to seek re-election in 1888. He was succeeded as president by Samuel Mellor of Jersey City. Mellor was a trade union man, but a "middle of the roader," preferring to have the Knights in rather than out of the Federation. John McCormack of Trenton became vice-president; Owen White, a member of the Knights from Paterson became secretary; and Henry Stokes was re-named treasurer. By 1888, the power of the Knights in the Federation had waned so far that the Federation probably joined the American Federation of Labor as a state affiliate.

In the next (1889) convention of the State Federation the strength of the Knights continued to decline, although Owen White was retained as secretary. Mellor remained as president. By 1890, the trade unionists were in such complete control that the credentials of two Knights assemblies were rejected including those of Owen White.

In confirmation of the triumph of the craft unionists over the Knights in New Jersey, Samuel Gompers, long-time foe of the Knights, came to address the convention of 1890. Speaking to the Federation of Trades and Labor Unions of New Jersey, Gompers referred to the struggle between the trades unions and the Knights and the victory of the former: "With pleasure I note that notwithstanding the antagonisms you have had to contend with, you are unwavering in your determination to maintain your organization." *

* *Newark Evening News,* Aug. 19, 1890.

Although there were a few more scuffles with the Knights in subsequent conventions, beginning with the meeting of 1890 the Federation was safely in the hands of the craft unionists, and the foundation of the modern union movement in New Jersey as an organization of skilled workers was secured. The organizations attending the 1890 Convention were nearly all craft, as indicated below.

TABLE 6

ORGANIZATIONS ATTENDING THE CONVENTION OF THE STATE
FEDERATION OF TRADES AND LABOR UNIONS, 1890 *

Name of Union	City	Member-ship
Typographical Union, Local 103	Newark	140
Cigar Makers	Newark	260
Carpenters and Joiners, Local 325	Paterson	104
Clothing Salesman's Assn.	Newark	61
Engineers	Jersey City	50
Cigar Makers Union	Jersey City	60
Carpenters and Joiners	Passaic	490
Progressive Musical Union	Paterson	31
Carpenters and Joiners, Local 482	Orange	26
Carpenters and Joiners, Local 573	Rutherford	23
Painters Protective Union	Paterson	50
Cigar Makers Union	Orange	26
Typographical Union, Local 8	Newark	45
Bakers Union, Local 2	Newark	47
Grocery and Tea Clerks Assn.	Newark	50
Typographical Union, Local 71	Trenton	110
Cigar Makers Union, Local 3	Paterson	80
Central Labor Union	Newark	—
Passaic County Trades Assembly	—	—
Building Trades Council of Hudson County	—	—
Total		1653

* Files of I. Kerrison, Special Mss Collections, New Jersey Room, Rutgers University Library.

In addition to the State Labor Congress, as previously noted, the Knights in their brief history in New Jersey also formed the Essex County Trades Assembly in 1880. According to its successor, the Essex (County) Trades Council, the Trades Assembly "during its history accomplished considerable good through its influence upon the subordinate bodies of workmen . . . [and that] the period of its existence witnessed a steady growth of union sentiment." *

The Assembly was re-organized in 1892 as the Essex Trades Council by eight trade unions; all eight were locals of national unions, showing how important national unions had become on the local scene.

The Council's activities included supporting member unions on strike, publishing lists of employers declared "unfair" to union labor, and promoted the use of the union label on goods made by unionized workers. It also joined the State Federation of Labor, probably in 1892 and like the Federation took a non-party approach to politics. The Council supported candidates of either party so long as the individual favored organized labor's programs.

Among the leading local unions in Newark affiliated with national organizations and the Essex Trades Council were Typographical Local 103, Cigar Makers Local 138, Electrical Workers Local 52, the German-American Typographical Local 8, the Newark Hat Makers (affiliated with the National Hat Makers Union of North America), the Metal Polishers, Buffers and Platers Local 44, Retail Clerks Local 206, and Printing Pressmen's Local 31.

McGuire and Labor Day

A labor leader, prominent on the national scene at the end of the nineteenth century who came to be identified with New Jersey, was Peter J. McGuire, Father

* Essex Trades Council, *Illustrated History of the Essex Trades Council* (Newark, 1899), 248.

Labor Day Parade in Newark, 1885
New York Daily Graphic, July 28, 1885
Courtesy of New Jersey Division, Newark Public Library

of Labor Day. Although born in New York in 1852, he apparently spent his last years in New Jersey, being buried in Arlington Cemetery, Camden.

McGuire helped to establish the present-day Brotherhood of Carpenters and Joiners Union, one of the largest national unions in the country. He served as the union's secretary-treasurer for over a quarter of a century. In addition to his organizational role in the Carpenters, he was among the founders of the American Federation of Labor.

Although once a Socialist, McGuire was one of the small number of labor leaders who swung union philosophy decisively toward accepting capitalism and the practice of business unionism, that is, improving the material lot of skilled workers through collective bargaining.

The idea of Labor Day, a day of recognition of the contribution of workers to American society and economic strength, was said to have been proposed by McGuire at a meeting of the Central Labor Union of New York in May of 1882. At that meeting he recommended that the unions seek official recognition of a holdiay falling between the Fourth of July and Thanksgiving Day to honor "the industrial spirit, the great vital force of the nation." * A dozen years later Congress made Labor Day a national holiday.

When McGuire died in 1904 in Camden, he was penniless. His funeral was small and virtually unnoticed except for a few friends in the union movement.

SOCIALISM

Another force which swept briefly into New Jersey, but unlike the Knights left no tangible results in union organization, was socialism. In politics, socialism's impact on the State was shown in the founding of the oldest socialist party in the United States, the Socialist Labor Party, organized in Newark in 1877.

* *Newark News,* Sept. 2, 1956.

Like many in labor, the Socialists were divided on the efficacy of the political versus the trade union method of advancing the interests of workers, but in New Jersey, the trade union viewpoint won out and led to the formation of the International Labor Union. Unlike the trade unions but similar to the Knights of Labor, the Socialists were anxious to organize the unskilled worker in the technologically advancing industries of manufacturing.

The philosophy of the union leadership as expressed by the union's president, George E. McNeill, was that labor and management should be left alone to work out their problems. Government intervention was opposed. In testimony before a Congressional committee seeking remedies to labor-management conflicts, McNeill stated that if the Committee "discovers that the troubles which workingmen complain of are world-old and God-ordained, or at least beyond the reach of any legislative panacea . . . a very important salutory influence upon the prevailing controversy will have been attained." *

The Socialists behind the International Labor Union turned their attention first to factory workers in cotton textiles. Although the International Labor Union originated in Fall River, Massachusetts, in 1878, Paterson became its center of strength. It was the first union of textile workers in the state. One of the important figures in the International Labor Union was Joseph P. McDonnell, a Socialist, who came to the forefront during an eight-month strike over wages by cotton textile workers in Paterson. He had previously moved his labor newspaper, the *Labor Standard,* from Fall River to Paterson, where it became labor's voice on labor issues and the official paper of the State AFL in 1890. One of the most notable examples of McDonnell's verbal fireworks occurred in the course of the aforementioned strike when in the second issue of the *Paterson Labor*

* Files of I. Kerrison, Special Mss Collections, New Jersey Room, Rutgers University Library.

Standard McDonnell labeled some strikebreakers "scabs."

He was tried for using the term "scabs," found guilty, and fined $500 and costs by Judge Barkalow of Paterson. Within two hours, his sympathizers raised the money to pay his fine. A great celebration in Paterson followed. The term "scab" thereafter became part of the lexicon of organized labor, although it had been known as far back as the 1790's.*

In 1879 McDonnell was back in court for publishing a worker's letter exposing the treatment of brickmakers in a Singac brickyard. The trial found McDonnell and the letter writer, Michael Menton, guilty. They were fined and sentenced to county jail. Upon his release, McDonnell was again lionized by the workers of Paterson.

The International Labor Union planned to send McDonnell to a meeting of the British Trades Union Congress in order to establish ties with the British union movement, but the trip failed to materialize because the union commenced a sharp decline into oblivion. By the end of 1878 it was said to have 8000 members but after a number of defeats in strikes, the ILU had shrunk to a single branch in Hoboken by 1881, and dissolved entirely by 1887.

McDonnell drifted from Socialist principles and became one of the organizers of the New Jersey Federation of Trades and Labor Unions in 1883. He was also elected chairman of its legislative (after 1890, the executive) committee for fifteen years. He also organized the trades assembly of Paterson in 1884 and was responsible for the first state law recognizing Labor Day, enacted by New Jersey in 1887.

Although national forces—the Civil War, the extension of markets, the rise of the national union movement—had some effect on New Jersey between 1860 and 1873, the first national organization to have a decisive influence in the state was the Knights of Labor. The

* See above, page 16.

first city, county, and state federations of labor in New Jersey were the result of the activities of the Knights.

The State Labor Congress of 1879, inspired and organized by the Knights, was succeeded in 1883 by the Federation of Organized Trades and Labor Unions. About 1888, this organization affiliated with the American Federation of Labor. Likewise the Essex County Trades Assembly, set up by the Knights in 1880, became the Essex Trades Council in 1892.

With the founding of the Congress in 1879 the modern union movement in New Jersey had started. The trade unions' rout of the Knights, completed by 1890, made it a movement limited to highly skilled workers, and it remained a movement limited to the skilled craftsmen until the New Deal. Likewise, on the national scene, the formation of the AFL in 1886 dates the national union movement, also predominately craft until the New Deal, from that year.

Socialist efforts to bring unions to the unskilled textile workers in 1878 were the first to have any success. However, their achievements were short lived.

Attempts to unionize the unskilled in New Jersey's textile industry continued with little success. In contrast, the skilled workers successfully built on the foundations laid down by 1890.

IV

THE MODERN UNION MOVEMENT
1890-1933

From its charter by the American Federation of Labor about 1888 until the rise of the New Deal in 1933, the growth of the State Federation, its affiliates, and other unions in New Jersey was largely determined by business conditions and World War I. Moreover, the union movement in New Jersey, like that of the nation, consisted primarily of skilled workers in the building, printing, and metal trades.

The principal differences between the industrial make-up of New Jersey's union movement and the Nation's were the greater preponderance of the building trades (the carpenters, bricklayers, electricians, painters, and plumbers) and the absence of coal unionism in New Jersey (owing to the lack of commercial coal deposits). Consequently, the dynamism of the United Mine Workers union and its leadership were not felt in local union affairs. Similarly, the two principal needle trades unions, the Amalgamated Clothing Workers and the International Ladies Garment Workers Union, both noted for their liberalism in politics and their pioneering in collective bargaining, had minor roles in New Jersey because of their relatively small memberships.

The dominance of the building trades unions had important political and economic consequences for unionism in New Jersey. More than any other factor, it explains the character and activities of the New Jersey

State Federation of Labor. In general, the building trades (and the metal and printing trades) unions are conservative in politics, and in the labor market favor limitations on the number of skilled workers to be admitted to membership, the number of workers to be employed in a given operation, and a ban on working with non-members.

For example, in 1907 a Hackensack local of the Bricklayers adopted a working rule containing the following clause:

That one bricklayer or mason, exclusive of superintendent or foreman to every seven laborers or less, be employed on all walls and footings of concrete. On floors, two bricklayers, masons or plasterers, to do all rodding. Screeding and all top dressing to be done by none but members of the Bricklayers Masons and Plasterers International Union of America.*

The problems of the production workers in manufacturing were remote from the union movement of the skilled. Consequently, they offered little if any effective leadership to the struggles of the factory worker for recognition and status. The two groups remained separate, and this differentiated the approach of each to industrial and political problems.

In contrast to the founding of a union movement among skilled workers in industries lagging technologically, workers in the technologically more advanced industries of the state, epitomized by textiles, met defeat in their efforts to unionize.

Indeed, the history of the modern union movement in New Jersey, until the rise of the CIO in the late 1930's, consisted of two movements: one, the successful unionization of the skilled workers, especially in building, metal trades, and printing; and, the second, the unsuccessful efforts to organize the unskilled, particularly in textiles.

* Harry C. Bates, *Bricklayer's Century of Craftsmanship* (Washington, 1955), 146.

THE STATE FEDERATION OF LABOR

The New Jersey State Federation of Labor, affiliated with the American Federation, became the representative of the union movement in the state, just as the AFL came to be identified as the center of unionism nationally. The State Federation came to occupy this position even though many local unions which belonged to the national AFL did not also affiliate with the State Federation. Unions outside, or independent of the AFL, likewise did not belong to the State Federation. Nevertheless, many of the leading organizations did join, making the Federation the authoritative voice of organized labor in this state. Consequently, we shall identify union trends to 1933 primarily with the fortunes of the New Jersey State Federation of Labor, AFL.

After the rout and expulsion of the remaining Knights of Labor groups from the Federation's Convention of 1890, the union movement declined steadily, but nevertheless stayed intact and began to revive by 1893. The Convention of 1891 had fewer delegates and organizations represented than in 1890; however it called for action to intensify union organization. First, it urged the affiliates to form city associations "to be composed exclusively of trade unions" (another attack on the fast-failing Knights), and second, it urged the parent AFL to pay the expenses of an organizer to be appointed by the State Federation. However, the national AFL, being in poor financial condition, was not able to meet this demand until 1902. Joseph P. McDonnell, who was appointed a general organizer of the AFL, was apparently paid by the New Jersey Federation.

Samuel Mellor, President of the Federation since 1888, was re-elected to that office in 1891. In the following year Thomas McGovern, a typographer from Local 103 in Newark became president. In 1893, a member of the Carpenters Union, Samuel Hold, of Paterson, was chosen president, suggesting the growing importance of the building-trades unions in the Federation. In line with the building trades' emphasis on exclusive jurisdiction, the Federation in 1893 revised its Constitution to include among its purposes the recognition of the strict autonomy of each trade.

Hold continued as president until 1895, when he was succeeded by William Yuile, a printer. Yuile resigned and his term was completed by William Marburger, the Federation's Vice-President. Marburger, another printer, was elected to the presidency in 1896, and re-elected until 1899. In that year, John A. Moffitt, a member of the Hatters' Union took office. In 1901, during Moffitt's administration, the Federation of Trades and Labor Unions of New Jersey changed its official name to the New Jersey State Federation of Labor.

With Moffitt's successor, Cornelius Ford, a printer, the Federation got the first of a number of long-term administrations, a feature characteristic of stable organizations and well-entrenched bureaucracy. Ford took office in 1902 and held the post until 1913. Meanwhile, the annual convention report, which heretofore had been made by the chairman of the executive committee, was now shared by the president and the secretary-treasurer.

The membership of the Federation was approximately 2000 in 1895, a figure exceeding the number in 1890. During the recession which began in 1896, the membership of the Federation dropped to under 1700. It rose to nearly 1800 in 1897 (Appendix C).

Thereafter, in the closing years of the nineteenth century, union organization began to pick up, and momentum carried it onward until the recession of 1904-1905.

In 1899, there was a successful strike of glass workers in Bridgeton, Clayton, Fairton, Elmer, Glassboro, Minotola, and Medford. Thousands flocked to the Glass Workers Union over the next two years as a result of the successful strike of 1899. The strike was directed against the employer's practice of paying wages in company script, redeemable only at company stores, and their opposition to unions.

The turn in the fortunes of the glass workers was shared by other groups such as carpenters, painters, and printers. The building trades of Hudson County won a strike for an eight-hour day, while lathers in Passaic made gains in wages.

Surveys by the Bureau of Statistics in 1899-1901, show that important gains were made by many unions, but that total union membership was probably still below the level of 1887. In 1901, total membership in the state stood at about fifteen thousand while in 1887 it had almost reached eighteen thousand. At the turn of the century about 2 per cent of the labor force of New Jersey were unionized, a ratio slightly below the national average.

Meanwhile, the increasing importance of craft unionism in the New Jersey movement was emphasized by two developments in the building trades. In 1899 what was left of the Knights of Labor in Hudson County conceded the exclusive right to organize painters and carpenters to the Hudson County Building Trades Council. Such a concession reveals the pre-eminence of the trades unions in these occupations, and probably marks the final local retreat of the Knights in their losing battle with the unions.

The second episode underlining the jealously guarded claims of the building craftsmen was the request of the Union County Trades Council in 1902 of the Electrical Trades Union of Newark that it relinquish its claim over the electricians of Elizabeth. If granted (and we don't know if it was), the Union County Trades Council could then turn their energies to organizing the electricians of Elizabeth. To do otherwise would be "dualism," that is, organizing workers claimed by another AFL union, and that was a serious offense for a trade union.

The State Federation's Convention of 1902 reported

that the year was one of growth for the movement, and listed 11 new organizations as applicants for charters. The Hudson County Central Labor Union reported 4 new affiliates, while the Essex Trades Council had a total of 19. In New Brunswick a Trades and Labor Federation was established, and in Camden 37 unions were reported affiliated with the Central Labor Union. The Convention of 1902 gave its support to the famous anthracite strike in neighboring Pennsylvania and urged government seizure of the mines to end the dispute.

Cornelius Ford, who succeeded John A. Moffitt in the Federation presidency in 1902, was re-elected annually until President Woodrow Wilson appointed him the Public Printer of the United States on June 26, 1913. He remained in that position for the eight years of the Wilson Administration, and then returned to New Jersey and union affairs. From 1910 to 1912 inclusive, Ford, a Democrat, served in the State Assembly. Ford's career as union official and politician was to be emulated many times over by leaders in the New Jersey union movement.

The growth of unions continued in 1903 as indicated by reports of the Federation. Membership of the Federation reached a record high of 17,600 in 1903. Seven new affiliates joined the Federation in 1903. Meanwhile, a new Central Labor Union was established in Atlantic City. The following year, the United Trades Council of Paterson was so well established in the city and environs that it was able to negotiate a master agreement with the Master Builders. In addition to wages, hours, and the like, the agreement (an annual one) provided for a joint board of arbitration.

The increase in the number of Federation affiliates in 1903 was part of a general upturn in union organization in the state. In 1903, as Table 7 shows, 55 new unions were organized, the largest number in any year before World War I.

However, the downturn of business in 1904-1905 checked the growth of New Jersey unions, with none being organized in 1905. The following year saw a revival in union organization along with the revival in business conditions.

The growth of unions prior to World War I led to an increased number of local associations throughout the state. Thus, in Trenton in 1906, a building trades council was set up, and in the same year, an association of unions in beer bottling was organized. In the following year, the Essex and Hudson counties Trades Councils joined with the Building Trades Councils of these areas to form central labor councils.

The metal trades, comprising such unions as the iron molders, metal polishers, and brass finishers, and the machinists joined together in 1908 to establish the Metal Trades Council of New Jersey. Its purposes were to establish local unions in each of the metal trades, the eight-hour day, and collective bargaining.

Beginning in 1909, with the election of Henry Hilfers as secretary of the Federation, a consistent body of information on the Federation became available. Hilfers was secretary to Local 138 of the Cigar Makers and to the Essex Trades Council before taking the same post with the Federation. Born in 1862, he followed his father in the trade of cigar-making and in his belief in unionism. Henry F. Hilfers served as Federation secretary for seventeen years, and Essex Trades Council secretary for twenty-two years.

After 1903, when the Federation's membership soared to over 17,000, it apparently lost ground under the depressions of 1904-1905 and 1907-1908. However, in most years from 1909 to 1914, the membership (Appendix C), number of unions affiliated and delegates attending the annual conventions increased. The recession of 1913-1914 temporarily reduced the strength of the Federation. During war years which followed, the State AFL gained increasing numbers and strength.

Arthur A. Quinn, of the Carpenters Union, who succeeded Cornelius Ford as president of the Federation in 1913, was the first of the building tradesmen to hold

TABLE 7

Unions Formed Annually in New Jersey *
1903-1916

	1903	1904	1905	1906	1907	1908
Building Trades	25	4		19	3	1
Transportation and communication	4			4		2
Manufacturing	21	6		11	2	
Food	1	1				
Paper products	2					
Machinery and metals	7			5		
Transportation equipment		1		1		
Rubber, clay and stone products	4			1	2	
Furniture and wood products	3					
Leather products						
Textiles	2			1		
Printing	1	4				
Apparel				2		
Miscellaneous	1			1		
Trade and Services	2			13	1	2
All Others	3			1	2	
Totals	55	10	0	48	8	5

* New Jersey Bureau of Statistics of Labor and Industry, *Annual Reports,* 1903-1916.

the presidency for a long term, continuing in office until 1933. He was succeeded by other long-term presidents from the building trades, notably Louis P. Marciante of the Electricians, and the incumbent president of the AFL-CIO, Vincent Murphy, of the Plumbers.

Like Ford, Quinn was a member of the Assembly, holding office from 1913 to 1915. In 1929 he was elected State Senator from Middlesex and served until 1933. Quinn was also elected first vice-president of the Brotherhood of Carpenters in 1913, and, had it not been for a quirk of fate, would have succeeded to the presidency of this national union, one of the largest and most

1909	1910	1911	1912	1913	1914	1915	1916	Total
	2	5	3	1		1	4	68
3		2				2	1	18
7	3		7	8	4	3	9	81
2	1			1	1			7
							1	3
	2			1	2	1		18
								2
3			1	1			1	13
								3
				1				1
1			3	1	1	2	2	13
								5
1			2	3			5	13
			1					3
4	2	2			2	1	5	34
				1		1		8
14	7	9	10	10	6	8	19	209

powerful in the AFL. Upon election to the vice-presidency of the Carpenters, he was supposed to move to the national headquarters in Indianapolis, but according to one account, he "did not relish the idea of abandoning his Bergen and Hudson County haunts to his [political] enemies in favor of a $1,600 a year job in the Middle West. Hence, on April 22 [1913], he begged off because of 'eye trouble' and Hutcheson assumed his job." * A year later the President of the Carpenters died and William Hutcheson instead of Arthur A. Quinn stepped into the job. Hutcheson retained the presidency for many years thereafter, and bequeathed the job to his son, Maurice Hutcheson.

* Robert A. Christie, *Empire in Wood* (Ithaca, 1956), 199.

By 1914 the union movement among skilled workers, especially in the building, metal, and printing trades, was firmly established in New Jersey. Nationally, total union membership rose by over two million between 1897 and 1914, increasing from 447,000 in 1897 to 2,687,000 in 1914. Proportionate expansion took place in New Jersey over the same period.

Industrial Warfare in Textiles

While the skilled craftsman was making steady if unspectacular gains in union organization, the unskilled and the semi-skilled in the states' manufacturing industries, notably textiles, were etching a record of sporadic and spectacular failures to unionize. The first strike of unskilled factory workers occurred in the cotton mills of Paterson in 1828; it grew from a protest of the workers and was not called by a union. This strike was followed by another in 1835, one in 1851, a series of unsuccessful stoppages in 1858-1859 in the wake of a depression, and still another strike by cotton textile operatives in 1878. The last was led by the International Labor Union, although beginning before the union appeared on the scene, a situation which was to be repeated on a number of historic occasions. The International Labor Union was the first union organization in New Jersey's textile industry.

By the end of the Civil War cotton textiles began to give way in importance to the silk industry.* The silk industry began in Paterson with a mill opened by a member of the Colt family in 1838. The factory, known as the "gun mill," was built in 1835 by the Patent Arms Manufacturing Company, of which Samuel Colt was head, for the production of Colt's revolvers and rifles. In 1838, Christopher Colt, a brother of Samuel Colt, transferred a small plant of crude silk machinery for thread-making from Hartford, Connecticut, to Paterson

* While Paterson became a silk center, Passaic attracted a growing wool-manufacturing industry.

and was allowed to place it on the top floor of the new building.

However, Christopher Colt's efforts failed, and the Colt plant was purchased by one George W. Murray. Murray put an English immigrant in charge, John Ryle, who for about a year earlier had been employed as a foreman in silk manufacture in Northampton, Massachusetts. Operations commenced with four workers. In 1846, Murray retired and sold his interests to Ryle, who gradually expanded and enlarged the business.

By the time of the Civil War there were still only four silk mills in the city of Paterson or its environs. However, the high tariffs enacted at this time fostered the growth of the industry. As of 1870, about two-thirds of the silk consumed in the country was imported, but by 1914, this was reduced to one-tenth. Output grew nine-fold with attendant growth in employment.

In the transition from cotton to silk,

the traditions of the labor movement that had become established among the cotton workers were shared by operatives in the silk industry. . . . A close internal relationship also existed among silk and cotton manufacturers, based upon their engagement in similar types of production in the same city.*

In addition, the silk industry was subject to the same type of product competition, improvements in technology, mobility of capital, and the extensive use of female, child, and immigrant labor, mostly unskilled, which had been characteristic of the cotton and woolen industries. Consequently, labor relations came to bear the same marks of instability, emotionalism, and at times violence that had characterized labor relations in the older textile industries. A new factor was the interest of revolutionaries, Syndicalists, Anarchists, and Communists, in the condition of the textile workers of

* James E. Wood, "History of Labor in the Broad-Silk Industry of Paterson, New Jersey, 1872-1940" (Unpublished doctoral dissertation, University of California, 1941), 136.

New Jersey. The appearance of the International Labor Union, Socialist in inspiration and organized on an industrial basis, was tame by comparison to the movements which followed in 1912, 1913, and 1926.

Like the early strikes of cotton textile operatives, those of the silk workers were also typically undertaken by the workers themselves without a union. Of 137 recorded strikes in the silk industry of New Jersey from 1881 to 1900, 78 were spontaneous while 59 were ordered by a union.*

The Knights of Labor followed the International Labor Union among silk workers, appearing in Paterson initially in 1879 with Pioneer Assembly 1280. It was followed by another assembly in 1885 and later that year, by three more locals. Together, the five organizations were formed into District Assembly 100. Most of the members were skilled workers from the silk and other industries—dye house operatives, ribbon and broad-silk workers, as well as machinists, ironworkers, flax workers, shirt-ironers, and molders.

Later, by 1887, the number of local assemblies in the Paterson area was gradually increased to 15, and the Knights' membership rose to nearly 3000. The newer members were predominately the unskilled and the foreign-born; more than a quarter were women. Because of their rapid growth, the Knights formed the Paterson silk membership into the short-lived National Silk Trades Assembly 222.

Like most Knights groups, those in silk also sought to avoid strikes, preferring negotiation. But despite the official opposition to strikes, the Dyers' Assembly did stage a walk-out in 1887. Although at first successful, the Dyers Assembly eventually lost the strike, and as a

* James E. Wood, "History of Labor in the Broad-Silk Industry of Paterson, New Jersey" (Unpublished doctoral dissertation, University of California, 1941), 160. Details which follow on union organization in the silk industry depend primarily on this dissertation.

result soon disappeared. Between 1887 and 1894 there was no organization among dyers.

Along with the general decline of the Knights, its assemblies in silk either disbanded or reorganized as local independent unions. Thus, Local Assembly 7098 withdrew and became the independent Silk Loomfixers and Twisters Benevolent and Protective Association, a small union of skilled workers which lasted into the twentieth century.

Following the disintegration of Knights of Labor, the typical form of union organization in silk came to be the local independent, a type of organization then disappearing among craft unions. In 1893 the independent United Silk Ribbon Weavers Association was organized, followed in 1894 by the Horizontal Warpers Benevolent Association.

The United Silk Ribbon Weavers launched a general strike for higher wages in 1894 that was unsuccessful, but was important because it had the attributes which came to be the hallmark of strikes in the state's textile industries: there were mass meetings, addresses by Socialists, Anarchists, and "do-gooders" translated into several languages, emotionalism (which included the singing of the "Marseillaise"), incidents between strikers and non-strikers, destruction of property, skirmishes with police, arrests, and suppression of civil liberties.

The local independent union movement was swelled with the formation of the United Broad Silk Workers Association in 1898, and culminated in a federation of independent silk unions, the United Silk Workers of America organized in 1901. A year later it changed its name to the Allied Silk Unions' Executive Board.

The Allied Silk Unions' Executive Board functioned about two years; its principal functions were to settle jurisdictional claims among associated unions and to coordinate policy toward employers. It conducted three strikes, all of which it lost. It was most successful in its promotion of a textile school where the various trades in silk were taught. However, this aroused the opposition of two affiliates, the Loomfixers and Twisters Union, and the Warpers Union, which expected to control entry into their trades, like the building and printing trades unions, and therefore regarded the school as a threat.

The Allied Silk Unions' Executive Board did little to organize and accomplished virtually nothing in politics. It was poorly financed and fell apart in 1903 when the two key unions, the Loomfixers and Twisters, and the Warpers, withdrew.

Prior to its dissolution, the Allied Silk Unions' Executive Board sought to affiliate with the AFL. However, in 1901 the AFL had granted a charter to the United Textile Workers of America which included jurisdiction over the silk industry, and the UTW refused to accept any reduction of its jurisdictional claim. Consequently, the AFL denied a separate charter to the Allied Silk Unions' Executive Board, although it alone represented any effective organization in the industry.

However, labor relations in silk were not all a matter of putting together and re-shuffling unions. On June 18, 1902, a strike of weavers in Paterson culminated in a mob attack on several silk mills in Paterson. William MacQueen, an alleged anarchist, was arrested, found guilty of inciting to riot and malicious mischief, and was sentenced to five years in the State prison. The riot followed a meeting addressed by MacQueen and two others. After the speech of one Galiano, the meeting erupted into a mob. It "attacked about ten mills and destroyed several thousand dollars worth of property." *
A number of persons were shot, although none were killed. Only MacQueen was apprehended; the strike ended in failure.

Syndicalism in two forms, direct action through strikes and sabotage to overthrow capitalism and peaceable political action, came to New Jersey's textile industries with the arrival of the Chicago and Detroit fac-

* Alfred W. Wishart, *The Case of William MacQueen* (Trenton, 1905), 6.

tions of the Industrial Workers of the World. In point of fact, neither group made serious inroads on the ideological convictions of workers, but they did provide the leadership and organization in New Jersey's textile industries which was not available from the American Federation of Labor, the United Textile Workers, AFL, or the New Jersey State Federation of Labor.

The Detroit, or political-action IWW group, opened a series of battles against employers in silk with a strike at the Doherty Company in Clifton over the issue of the workload, specifically on the number of looms each worker would tend. The transition from hand to power looms was well under way by the middle of the 1880's, and as further improvements were made, workers were given additional machines to operate. By 1905, the hand loom was virtually extinct being replaced by automatic-stop looms. In 1886 two looms per worker was the standard, when only a few years before one was typical. In 1910, the Doherty Company's new plant in Clifton was set up to increase the work assignment to three and four looms.

Meanwhile, New Jersey silk producers were facing intensive competition, particularly from northeastern Pennsylvania, where a substantial part of the industry had begun to migrate chiefly to take advantage of lower labor costs. In Pennsylvania three and four looms were becoming standard, and child labor was still widely used. New Jersey, in contrast, had substantially elimi-nated child labor in factories, workshops, and mines since the Stainsby Act of 1883. In addition, a New Jersey law of 1892 limiting hours to 55 per week in silk manufacture kept women workers' hours below those in Pennsylvania. Finally, wages were lower in Pennsyl-vania. Significantly, there are no data for men's wage scales in Pennsylvania or for children in New Jersey. This indicates that while men were widely employed in New Jersey, they were not in Pennsylvania. The reverse was true of child labor.

The United Textile Workers, AFL, which had come

to represent the Doherty workers, accepted the three- and four-loom workload but the workers did not. They withdrew from the UTW in November, 1911, and joined the Industrial Workers of the World, Detroit faction.

Generally, it can be said that although the Paterson silk workers' "long history of militant action had prepared them adequately for acceptance of such leadership . . . [their] ready response . . . to IWW leadership in 1911-1912 demonstrated their dissatisfaction with the U.T.W. policies." *

The silk strike in Paterson began on February 23, 1912, spreading to include 5000 weavers, women and men, in 120 mills in and around Paterson. Nevertheless the mills operated at about one-third of capacity. The stoppage was extended to Plainfield, Summit, Hoboken, Bayonne, and to New York. Most shops were settled early in March, 1912 with wage gains, but some strikes were resumed when employers went back on their agreements. By May of 1912 most silk shops were again settled with some wage gains, but no union recognition, and therefore no consolidation of the improvements. As for the Doherty Company, it apparently accepted a modification of the three-and four-loom assignment.

In March, 1912, the Detroit IWW also led a strike of woolen workers in Passaic, Clifton, and Garfield. However, the Chicago group moved in to seize leadership in Garfield, after which the strike became violent. However, this strike brought no lasting positive results either.

The settlements of 1912 were broken when the Doherty weavers again struck over a renewal of the three-and four-loom assignment. This time, the conflict developed into a veritable general strike commanded by the Syndicalist, Chicago faction of the IWW. The strike began in earnest at the end of February, 1913, and lasted into July, officially terminating in defeat on August 1, 1913.

* James E. Wood, "History of Labor in the Broad-Silk Industry of Paterson, New Jersey" (Unpublished doctoral dissertation, University of California, 1941), 243.

An attempt by the United Textile Workers to re-enter the situation ended in fiasco: the workers preferred the dramatic, effective leadership of the IWW. No cooperation between the UTW and the IWW was possible, for "the UTW yielded to no one—not even the employers —in its hatred of this swift-moving, hard striking group which appealed primarily to the unskilled and unorganized foreign-born of the industry." *

During the strike, the Building Trades Council and the United Trades and Labor Council of Paterson offered their assistance to bring the strike to an end, but were spurned by the IWW in classic Syndicalist-Marxist reasoning and in typical language.

Although violence was rare in the great silk strikes of 1912 and 1913, they were distinguished by widespread violation of civil rights. One Valentino Modestino, a strike sympathizer, was shot in the back and killed while entering his house. Some fifteen thousand persons attended the funeral. A New Jersey law prohibiting incitement to riot was promiscuously used against the Chicago IWW and its leaders in 1913. During the strike over 2300 persons were arrested, 300 held for action of the grand jury, and more than 100 sentenced to imprisonment. Meanwhile, the workers, adopting a practice started in Italy, sent 5000 children away for safety and thereby embarrassed the community.

The 1913 strike was notable too for the personalities who were involved—"Big Bill" Haywood, John Reed, Elizabeth Gurley Flynn, Carlo Tresca, and Adolph Lessig—a who's who of the extreme left in the United States.

For the silk workers, the drama and notoriety brought no tangible, positive results, particularly in terms of permanent organization. As we shall see, they continued to seek unionization unsuccessfully for yet another quarter of a century.

* Herbert J. Lahne, *The Cotton Mill Worker* (New York, 1944), 200-201.

HUNGRY BABIES! - HUNGRY MOTHERS!

HUNGRY MEN!

FIVE MONTHS ON STRIKE AT PATERSON

Workers: —

Attention! Twenty five thousand of your fellow workers have been on strike for four months, since February 25th, struggling with all possible vigor and class conscious solidarity; meeting violence, all forms of brutality, prison and hunger in order to gain more bread, more life, more leisure, more light in their lives.

They were born in different lands, they speak different languages, profess different faiths but are now united in one great body in the cause of justice and brotherhood.

Why did they strike? We can tell you in a few words. Because the blood sucking capitalist monster had gone beyond all limits in exacting speed and the workers with starvation staring them in face and revolt burning in their hearts, preferred to strike and demand the abolition of the four loom sistem.

In years past the textile workers were running only one loom each and were working fairly good wages but after a while they were obliged to attend to two looms, and finally to three and four.

If salaries had only increased in proportion to the work! But far from it!

Fifteen years ago a weaver worked an 18-inch loom and received, for taffeta, 10 cents a yard. Now, he works four of them, 36 inches wide, ande receives only 2½ cents a yard.

Five years ago a weaver working two 36 inchs looms received, for musoline, 11½ cents a yard. Now, working four of them, receives only 5 cents a yard.

By working two looms, a weaver managed to make 30 yards of musoline a day, receiving thereby a compensation of $3.45. Now, working four looms, he can hardly make 48 yards a day and receives a compensation of $2.40. In other words, he produces 18 yards more and receives $1.05 a day less.

This is the reason for the strike: — the work has increased, the wages have decreased. And the greedy mill owners, never satisfied in their mad race for profits were intent on continuing this process indefinitely. "What are we to do? The weavers asked themselves on Feb. 25 — "Let us strike!" answered a chorus of thousands of voices. And since that day the police have been brutally beating men and women, the judges have handed down sentences on trumped up charges and sent to jail by the hundred, fathers, mothers, and even girls of tender years.

In Paterson injustice reigns supreme. Every constitutional right has been suppressed or violated by the contemptitle servile local authorities.

But the workers have resisted gallantly and are determined to win their battle. Only one enemy threatens, looming up at their very doors: HUNGER.

They have fought eighteen weeks! all reserve funds are now exhausted.

HELP! HELP! Workingmen help your Paterson brothers and sisters.

One for all and all for one! Give your mite, give your contribution of solidarity to the Paterson strikers. Make the struggle of the 25,000 Paterson strikers your struggle, their cause, your cause. Make their defeat your defeat and their victory your victory.

Send all contributions to — Silk Strikers Relief Committee,

HELVETIA HALL - Paterson, N. J.

Nicoletti Bros. Press, 242 Lafayette St., New York.

The onset of World War I did not immediately bring gains to unions in this country. In fact, there was a small decline in 1915. But thereafter, unions increased their numbers, with the tempo accelerating upon America's entry into the war and continuing until 1920, when membership reached a peak in excess of five million. The overall gain in the total membership of American unions from 1914 to 1920, about 2,300,000, nearly doubled the size of the union movement. Most of the increase went to established unions in coal mining, railway transportation, construction, shipbuilding, metalworking, and apparel.

The wartime upswing in unionism was felt in New Jersey, especialy among the building and the metal trades. The Federation, which in 1913 began a twenty-year-long period of administration by Arthur Quinn, saw its rolls of affiliates and members increase under the influence of World War I. Membership advanced from 18,700 in 1914 to 31,000 in 1920.

The year 1915 recorded more unions and delegates at the annual convention than ever before. Further increases in delegates and unions attending the annual conventions were registered in the period from 1916 to 1920.

At the 1916 Convention, Samuel Gompers once again addressed the delegates of the Federation; the last occasion was the 1890 meeting. Now he stressed the gains organized labor could expect from the passage of the Clayton Act of 1914. Gompers declared,

. . . that the labor of a human being is not a commodity or article of commerce. In other words, the old concept that the labor of a human being was the same as any profit from coal, iron, steel, wood, a side of pork, anything was the same as the labor of a human being—the labor power which consists in the mind and in the heart and the body, and that under the ill construction of the courts in their decisions

[made] . . . the same as a commodity. We have stuck a pin in that. That is the law.*

For nearly thirty years more, however, the courts did not adopt Gompers' views of the Clayton Act.

In 1917 the Federation resolved to establish a permanent office, in association with the independent railway unions, to lobby for favorable legislation in the assembly and senate. The following year, the Federation opposed conscription of labor to insure uninterrupted production, and expressed concern that a state anti-loafing law might be used to arrest strikers.

The war also stimulated unionism in textiles, as it did in the well-organized industries of the state. However, the Industrial Workers of the World did not share in the revival of textile organization. Indeed, by 1919 it had ceased to be a factor in the industry. On the other hand, the United Textile Workers of America, AFL, re-entered the state and organized some locals and a textile council.

Nevertheless, worker dissatisfaction with the UTW led to the formation of two new independent unions, the Amalgamated Textile Workers of America and the Associated Silk Workers. The Amalgamated was left-wing in orientation but rejected the Syndicalist philosophy of the IWW, as well as the conservative, business union approach of the UTW, AFL. In 1919 the Amalgamated and the Associated conducted strikes which were generally successful in reducing the work week to 44 hours and gaining higher wages.

Perhaps one of the most interesting developments to come out of the First World War for New Jersey was the growth of employee representation plans in Standard Oil and other leading employers in the State. While these were initiated by the companies, they were stimulated by the government's policy from 1917 to 1919

* *Proceedings of the 38th Annual Convention of the New Jersey State Federation of Labor,* Aug. 21-23, 1916, 15.

of setting up shop committees to carry out government-approved wage and hour changes and to adjust grievances in unorganized companies.

At Standard's Bayonne Refinery, the employee relations plan also grew out of a deteriorated labor relationship following a strike in 1915, in which the state militia was called out. The purpose of the plan was to provide systematic procedures and techniques to adjust grievances; it was not, however, collective bargaining. Since it did not require collective bargaining and yet, along with improved working conditions and rates of pay, produced such satisfactory results, the company instituted similar plans at its other installations throughout the country.

More significantly, Standard's success encouraged numerous other companies to set up employee representation plans, so that in the twenties, and again in the thirties, when the plans were converted into company unions, they became an important barrier and rival to trade unions.

POSTWAR DECLINE, 1920-1933

From a peak of more than five million members in 1920, the American trade union movement lost in excess of two million members by 1933. In that year it dropped below three million, a level just above the total membership in 1916, the year before America entered World War I. Because the economy, excepting agriculture, was operating at high levels of employment throughout much of the period, the loss of membership was highly unusual. Typically, unions had done well in periods of good business.

Among the factors responsible for the decline were the employers' drive to uproot the wartime growth of unionism, the reconversion of war industries to peace-time production and employment levels, the short but severe recession of 1921-1922, the depression of 1929-

1933, the inadequacy of the AFL's approach to the organization of manufacturing industries, and finally, the attitude of government.

The general decline in 1920-1921 hit New Jersey's union movement, too, but with much less impact than it hit the country as a whole. After dropping nearly 6,000 members between 1920 and 1921, the state Federation's membership remained virtually unchanged between 1921 and 1922. Thereafter it generally rose until 1928, in contrast to national trends which were down.

Doubtless, this stability may be attributed to the high proportion of building trades unionists in the Federation: there was a big building boom in the twenties, so unlike most other union groups, those in construction gained rather than lost in this period. With the depression of 1929-1933, the union movement in New Jersey declined with the rest of the unions in the country.

So successful was the staying power of the New Jersey union movement during the twenties, that in 1923 the Federation came out for the establishment of banks owned and operated by the unions. There was, at this time, a wave of interest in banking by organized labor, but many of the banks labor established subsequently failed.

A committee including Arthur A. Quinn, President, Henry Hilfers, Secretary, and Henry Carless, Counsel of the Federation, investigated the proposal and recommended its adoption. They concluded that workers needed a bank where their problems would be understood, and unbiased advice would be easily available.

As a result, the Union National Bank was chartered in April, 1925. Located in Newark, it began operating in June of the following year with a capitalization of $250,000 and $125,000 in surplus. Over 80 per cent of the stock was owned by organized labor. The bank was successfully managed through the financial panic and depression of 1929-1933. Later it was renamed the Broad National Bank. Today the Broad National Bank is the only bank in New Jersey known to recognize a union of its employees and deal with them through collective bargaining.

While this was the most impressive and successful of the union's banking efforts in New Jersey, the first labor bank in the State was organized in 1924 in Paterson primarily through the efforts of a few silk weavers. The trades unionists of Paterson were apathetic or negative in their response.*

The last labor bank in the eastern part of the country was set up in 1926 in Jersey City, largely as a result of the efforts of Theodore ("Terry") Brandle, of the Iron-workers Union. Both the Labor National Bank of Jersey City and the Paterson labor bank went bankrupt during the depression of 1929-1933.

Brandle, a political ally of Mayor Frank Hague of Jersey City, sought to gain control of the State Federation in 1925, but the combined voting of Essex and South Jersey re-elected Quinn to the presidency. Cornelius Ford, back in New Jersey union affairs, also played a role in repulsing Brandle and Hague.

Quinn continued in office until 1933 when he stepped down. He was succeeded for the year 1933-1934 by Thomas B. Eames, a member of the Glass Bottle Blowers Union.

Eames' election was sharply contested by two other candidates, and as a result, Eames won by a plurality of only 36 votes over the second-place runner, Louis P. Marciante of the powerful International Brotherhood of Electrical Workers. The close vote apparently engendered some resentment among Marciante's supporters, as reflected by a sudden and precipitous drop in the Federation's average paid membership. While the paid membership averaged 36,700 in 1933 at the bottom of the depression, it suddenly fell to 13,000 in 1934, a year of economic improvement. In 1935 membership returned

* Industrial Relations Section, Princeton University, *The Labor Banking Movement in the United States* (Princeton, 1929), 49.

to the 1933 number, after Marciante unseated Eames for the presidency of the state federation in the fall of 1934. His margin of victory over Eames was 16 votes.

DISINTEGRATION OF TEXTILE UNIONISM

While the union movement of skilled workers survived and even prospered in New Jersey during the 1920's, the textile unions brought into being during the First World War gradually fell apart. The Amalgamated Textile Union, a product of the war period, lost members and local units. Some of the locals joined the Associated Silk Workers, another union born during the war.

The battering of the 1920-1921 depression was so bad that by 1922 there was only a remnant left of the textile unions, the Amalgamated Textile Union, the Associated Silk Workers, and the United Textile Workers, affiliated with the American Federation of Labor.

In 1922, the Amalgamated Textile Union launched a federation of textile unions, but the effort eventually proved ineffectual and the federation disbanded in 1927. The Amalgamated itself went out of existence as a separate organization in 1923, leaving only the Associated Silk Workers and the United Textile Workers, AFL.

In 1926, the leading woolen mills of Passaic, Clifton, Garfield and Lodi were shaken by another of the dramatic strikes which had marked the history of New Jersey's textile industry. Indeed, the strike of 1926 was probably the outstanding labor conflict of President Calvin Coolidge's administration and was the "first great Communist strike in the United States." *

However, the intrusion of the Communist Party into

* Theodore Draper, *American Communism and Soviet Russia* (New York, 1960), 223, quoted in Esther Liberman, "The Influence of Left-Wing Radicalism in the Paterson Silk Strikes of 1912-1913, and the Passaic Woolen Strike of 1926" (an unpublished Mss in the author's possession), 34.

Details on this strike depend primarily on Esther Liberman's Mss, and on Morton Siegel, "The Passaic Textile Strike of 1926" (an unpublished doctoral thesis in Columbia University Library).

the leadership of the strike was virtually an accident: if the Communist Party had strictly followed the prevailing Party line, they should not have been in the forefront, as they came to be. But an intellectual who had recently converted to Communism, Alfred Weisbord, and the force of circumstances pushed the Party into this "awkward" position.

Orthodox Communist dogma toward American unions during the first half of the 1920's was a policy of "boring from within," that is, attempting to capture the unions by infiltration. At its Fourth Convention in August 1925, just prior to the strike, the Communist Party of the United States (then known as the Workers' Party) came out in favor of organizing textile workers by "strengthening the existing organizations" although leaving a loop-hole by adding that it also suported "the creation of new unions where none existed." In textiles, however, there was a functioning union, the United Textile Workers of America, AFL. Hence, the Party would deviate from its official line if it sponsored another labor organization. Yet, that is what the Communist Party did in the Passaic textile strike of 1926.

The strike broke out at the Botany Mills in January 1926 over wages, hours, and recognition of the United Front Committee, a Communist organization led by Alfred Weisbord. Botany had reduced wages by ten per cent in September 1925, contending that only in this way could the company continue to keep all employees on the pay roll. At first, Botany met no resistance from the workers, although Weisbord was able to enroll some workers in his United Front Committee of Textile Workers of Passaic and Vicinity. Later, however, in January 1926, members of the Committee approached management to demand restoration of the wage cut, time and a half for overtime, and recognition of the United Front Committee as the representative of the Botany workers. The company replied by firing the Committee members. Their discharge was immediately followed by a walk-out of some 5,000 Botany workers.

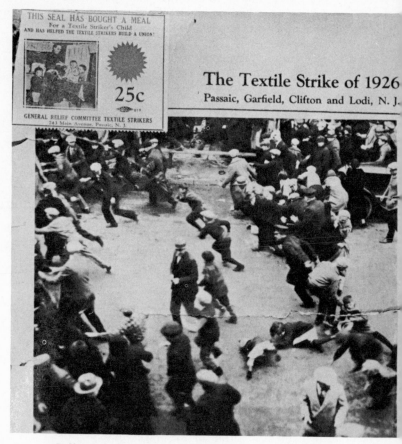

THIS SEAL HAS BOUGHT A MEAL
For a Textile Striker's Child
AND HAS HELPED THE TEXTILE STRIKERS BUILD A UNION!

25c

GENERAL RELIEF COMMITTEE TEXTILE STRIKERS
743 Main Avenue, Passaic, N. J.

The Textile Strike of 1926
Passaic, Garfield, Clifton and Lodi, N. J.

Police Attack on Demonstrators, Textile Strike of 1926
Courtesy of Mr. Frank Liberti

Shortly thereafter, in February, the strike spread to other mills and to the nearby communities of Clifton, Garfield, and Lodi. Employees of Forstmann and Huffman, New Jersey Worsted, Passaic Worsted, United Piece Dye Works and Dundee Textile went out on strike bringing the total number of strikers to over 10,000. New demands were now made on the Botany management: a wage increase of ten per cent above the levels of September 1925, compensation for the wages lost due to the wage reduction, a forty hour week, sanitary working conditions, and no discrimination in the rehiring of strikers.

Although technically placed in command of the strike by the Chairman of the Executive of the Workers' Party, Weisbord became its leader and hero by acclaim of the striking workers. They referred to him as "Jescusko," or little Jesus, because of his devotion to their cause. Alfred Weisbord was a graduate of the City College of New York, a member of Phi Beta Kappa, and a graduate of the Harvard Law School, class of 1924. He had been attracted to Socialism by 1920, and later to Communism. Within the Party, he supported the theory of dual unionism, the policy which the Workers' Party of the United States had rejected on orders from Moscow. Prior to the strike, Weisbord worked in a silk mill in Paterson, meanwhile organizing the United Front Committee as an instrument to conduct strikes. From the outset then, Weisbord was in conflict with the Party's supreme principle, unreserved acceptance of the Party line.

Weisbord's conduct of the strike was applauded by many including Henry F. Hilfers, secretary-treasurer of the New Jersey State Federation of Labor, and a foe of Communism. Hilfers said of Weisbord's leadership in the strike that, "he has accomplished what probably others couldn't. . . . He has kept the strikers out for a solid eight months. . . . I want to take my hat off to him.*

Unlike the Paterson silk strike of 1912 and 1913, the Passaic woolen strike of 1926 was marked by violence,

* *Proceeding of the New Jersey State Federation of Labor, 1926,* 65.

most of it by the police. On March 2, 1926 the police used tear gas and clubs to enforce an order banning picketing issued by the Commisioner of Public Safety of Passaic. The *Jersey City Journal* characterized the police as giving "the impression that they are a bunch of 'Cossacks.'" * However, police action went further than attacking the strikers; they also used force against out-of-town newspaper reporters and photographers who were giving publicity to the strike.

The strikers also resorted to force against non-strikers, although Weisbord opposed their actions. Nevertheless, personal attacks on non-strikers and bombings of their homes mounted as the strike wore on and the situation of the strikers grew more desperate.

Strike relief was given the United Front Committee by some sympathetic unions, churches and individual sympathizers. In June, 1926, when the relief funds were running low, the president of the Massachusetts Federation of Labor, AFL called for an end to AFL contributions because he claimed that the workers were being used to further communist propaganda.

Efforts to settle the strike by the Secretary of Labor, James J. Davis, and later the Governor of New Jersey, A. Harry Moore, were unsuccessful. In August, arrangements were made to ease Weisbord out of the strike and to turn the strike over to the United Textile Workers, AFL. However, the employers refused to bargain with any union and it was only through the mediation of local citizens that the strike was ended.

Limited agreement was obtained from Botany to re-employ strikers without discrimination. In general, the working conditions prevailing before the strike were reinstated. The only exception was an agreement to rescind the ten per cent wage cut, the issue which had precipitated the strike.

By September, the workers began to drift back to the

* Esther Liberman, "The Influence of Left-Wing Radicalism in the Paterson Silk Strikes of 1912-1913, and the Passaic Woolen Strike of 1926" (unpublished Mss in the author's possession), 38.

mills; they returned *en masse* on November 12, 1926 following an agreement worked-out between local residents and clergy with the Passaic Worsted Company. The strike ended completely on February 28, 1927 when workers in Lodi, the last holdouts returned to work.

The Communists remained, however, and with a change in the Party line of "boring from within" to dualism (setting-up unions to organize workers within the jurisdiction of existing unions), they organized locals in New Jersey of the Communist-sponsored National Textile Workers Union. However little headway was made, and unions in silk and wool alike declined during the depression of 1929-1933.

The modern union movement of New Jersey, embodied in the Federation of Organized Trades and Labor Unions, AFL, settled down to steady growth by the end of the nineteenth century. In 1901 the Federation changed its name to the New Jersey State Federation of Labor. It was a movement limited primarily to skilled workers in the building, metal, and printing trades. To a great extent the trend of its growth was influenced by business conditions and World War I. During the 1920's when unions in the country were losing members rapidly, the union movement in New Jersey apparently at least stabilized its position, if it did not run counter to the trend. The depression of 1929-1933, however, greatly reduced the size of the union movement in New Jersey, as it did in the Nation.

The stability of the Federation was reflected in the long administrations of two presidents, Cornelius Ford, 1902-1913, Arthur A. Quinn, 1913-1933, and Henry Hilfers' long secretaryship, from 1909 to 1926.

While the skilled workers were firmly establishing the roots of their unions, the unskilled (and even the skilled) in the state's textile industry repeatedly failed to do likewise. Dramatic strikes led by the Industrial Workers of the World were conducted in the silk industry in 1912 and 1913, and by the Communists in wool, in 1926-1927.

The State AFL and local union associations extended their sympathies to the strikers, but their support was minor and peripheral. Instead of the conservative leadership of the AFL, the textile workers turned to Syndicalists, Anarchists, Socialists, and Communists. But despite the fireworks provided by their colorful leadership, no permanent unions came out of these struggles.

At the depth of the depression, in 1933, there was virtually no unionism in textiles, but a strong if temporarily reduced union movement in the New Jersey building, metal, and printing trades.

V

THE NEW DEAL TO THE NEW FRONTIER
1933-1964

THE DEPRESSION of 1929-1933 shrank the union move-movent in the country to the membership level, more or less, of 1916. Likewise, the unions in New Jersey also declined during the severe depression, but apparently not so drastically as the national movement.

From this nadir of their fortunes, the national and New Jersey unions staged a revival and an expansion unprecedented in the annals of American labor organization. Of the new developments, two were outstanding: the unionization of the unskilled, primarily by unions affiliated with the Committee for Industrial Organization, known as the Congress of Industrial Organizations beginning in 1938; and, second, the Federal Government's venture into labor relations on a scale heretofore unknown in this country.

For New Jersey these developments meant extensive unionization of textiles, something that had eluded the industry since the first cotton mill strike in 1828. In addition, most workers in the state's other manufacturing industries, electrical machinery, fabricated metal products, chemicals, petroleum, and automobiles also became unionized. Meanwhile, the older unions of skilled workers in building, metal trades, and printing recouped their losses and went on to new records in numbers and economic strength.

Despite the organization of large numbers of production workers in manufacturing, the ideological if not the material gap persisted between the older craft unions and the newer CIO unions. Moreover, the greater preponderance of the building trades unions in this state in comparison to many other states, probably accentuated the rift between the "labor aristocracy" and the "labor masses" and their respective state federations. The rift showed up in differences between AFL and CIO trade union practices, philosophies, political approaches, and personalities. Furthermore, the rift continues to persist despite the nominal unity which prevails, and if one is to appreciate the position of organized labor in New Jersey, this fact must be recognized and accepted.

The question which arises is, why did not or could not the AFL and its unions organize the "labor masses"? The principal reasons were the AFL's craft approach to organizing the unorganized, its attitude and practices toward the unskilled and semiskilled worker, the Federation's general inexperience in dealing with the problems of factory workers, the lack of determination or desire to muster the manpower and financial resources necessary to unionize millions of production workers, and finally, a leadership whose philosophy was more attuned to the static technology of the skilled trades rather than the continuously changing processes of manufacturing.

Because of its overriding concern with craft lines and exclusive jurisdiction, the AFL usually insisted that its affiliates' claim to the unorganized crafts and occupations be settled in advance of any large-scale organizing campaign. In a sense, there had to be a division of the "spoils of war" before the first battle was fought.

To the mass production worker this zealous concern over craft jurisdiction seemed a poor way to enroll large numbers of assemblyline workers quickly and effectively. Moreover, the craft unions were concerned only about the skilled occupations and appeared to pay little regard, if any, to the great majority of semiskilled and unskilled workers.

High initiation fees and discriminatory practices alienated many unskilled laborers, semiskilled machine operators, women and negroes. The ineffectual approach of the craft unions to organizing large groups of workers in the great manufacturing companies of the nation made even the employer-sponsored union an alternative form of labor organization. Prior to the 1930's, many trade unions opposed or failed to appreciate the shop committee in a manufacturing plant as a means of settling issues and adjusting disputes. Differences in industrial relations practices among industries and plants were overlooked or ignored.*

Significantly, the faction within the AFL which favored organizing plants and companies without regard to the occupations of the workers were mostly leaders of industrial unions who were young or at the peak of their maturity. When they split apart from the AFL, the Commitee for Industrial Organizations and its successor, the Congress of Industrial Organizations, mobilized men and money to organize the unorganized on a scale that made previous AFL efforts puny by comparison.** It would be no exaggeration to say that the CIO was the first of the "big-time spenders" in the history of American labor.

John L. Lewis of the United Mine Workers led the group of unions within the AFL who urged a reformation in the Federation's approach to organizing. The New Deal Administration of President Franklin D. Roosevelt which gave organized labor the best prospects it had ever had to extend unionization made his proposals timely and urgent.

Under Section 7 (a) of the National Industrial Recov-

* William M. Leiserson, "Company Unions," in the *Encyclopedia of the Social Sciences* (New York, 1942), IV, 124.
** Walter Galenson, *The CIO Challenge to the AFL* (Cambridge, 1960), 595-601.

ery Act of 1933, declaring that workers had a legal right to join unions, the United Mine Workers, the International Ladies Garment Workers, the Clothing Workers, and the Teamsters made substantial gains. In 1935, passage of the Wagner Act presaged even greater governmental support for organizing unions.

Flushed with success, Lewis formed a Committee for Industrial Organization after the annual AFL convention in Atlantic City in 1935. At the convention, the AFL voted against unionization on industrial lines, so Lewis formed the CIO on his own initiative and against the wishes of the AFL.

Associated with Lewis and the Mine Workers were Sidney Hillman of the Amalgamated Clothing Workers, David Dubinsky of the International Ladies Garment Workers, and Charles Howard, President of the International Typographical Union. Howard joined on a personal basis and the union did not leave the AFL when the CIO broke with the Federation. The Committee pressed the leadership of the AFL to accept organization of the mass production industries on an industrial basis, without regard to occupation, but to no avail. The AFL leadership ordered the CIO to halt its plans for organizing on an industrial basis and then suspended the CIO unions which elected to persist in their plans. In October, 1937, the CIO, following its suspension by the Executive Committee of the AFL, elected John L. Lewis as Chairman of the Committee and set out to organize on an industrial basis. In the following year, the Committee was reorganized as the Congress of Industrial Organizations.

As part of their organizational plans, the CIO formed state groups to organize workers and to engage in political activity. The New Jersey Industrial Union Council was the twenty-fourth state association set up by the CIO. It was organized in the same year as the founding of the Congress itself, in October, 1938, claiming a membership at that time of 35,000. For about a year prior to the founding of the Industrial Union Council,

CIO Organizers in Jersey City, 1937

the CIO operated in New Jersey through a regional office headed by Wiliam J. Carney of the Mine Workers and later the Rubber Workers. Carney became the first president of the IUC, a post he held until his death in 1940.

ORGANIZATION IN TEXTILES, 1933-1940

The first industry in New Jersey to feel the effect of the new organizational drives of the CIO was textiles. As we have seen, textiles, had a long and unsuccessful record of union efforts to organize, and of that by 1933 only vestiges remained.

However, in 1934, textile unionism revived in New Jersey as a result of a nation-wide walkout called by the United Textile Workers, AFL. The strike which lasted three weeks engulfed over 400,000 workers in all parts of the country, despite the fact that at most the union had only 20,000 dues-paying members at this time.

The strike began in cotton on September 2, after the National Recovery Administration's approval of an industry proposal to reduce working hours to 30 per week with no change in wage rates, thus restricting the power of workers to earn up to the full weekly minimum possible under the code, $13 in the North and $12 in the South.* It soon spread to all parts of the textile industry, both North and South. In Paterson, a proposed strike of dyers was stopped by court injunctions when 20,000 writs were served individually. Nevertheless, thousands of silk workers did go on strike in northern New Jersey. One of the devices which made their strike effective was the use of "flying squadrons," that is, groups of workers moving from place to place in automobiles to induce non-strikers to leave their work. Of course, the antiquity of many of the cars made the term "flying squadrons" something of an exaggeration.

The strike ended on September 22 when President Roosevelt announced approval of the findings of a board

* Lewis L. Lorwin and Arthur Wubnig, *Labor Relations Boards* (Washington, 1935), 416.

which had examined the complaints of the textile workers. The President expressed his desire that the workers return to their jobs, and that the employers take them back without discrimination pending implementation of the report. However, the board's report did little more than recommend that other government groups handle and study the problems of textile labor, so few tangible results were realized. The purposes of the strike were therefore defeated, and a major reason for this was the weakness of the United Textile Workers, AFL.

Consequently, the UTW leadership viewed John L. Lewis' Committee for Industrial Organization as offering prospects for saving and strengthening the union. In 1937, the UTW came to terms with Lewis and Hillman and accepted a subordinate role in a new CIO organizational device, the Organizing Committee. The Textile Workers Organizing Committee was primarily financed and led by Sidney Hillman's Amalgamated Clothing Workers.

The contributions of the Clothing Workers, the Mine Workers and the Ladies Garment Workers Union to the Textile Workers Organizing Committee was stressed by the TWOC's first regional director in New Jersey, Carl Holderman:

It is a fact that the organizations such as the United Mine Workers, the Amalgamated Clothing Workers, and the International Ladies Garment Workers, who have contributed through assessments to finance the TWOC drive is itself a monument to their union ideals to build up a foundation for the benefit of the Textile Workers.*

In addition to spending large sums of money, the CIO built up impressive staffs of organizers and concentrated their resources in a massive drive on one or a

* *Minutes of the New Jersey State Joint Board*, Textile Workers Organizing Committee, 27 Nov., 1937, 11. Most of what follows on the organization of the TWOC in New Jersey is from these minutes, made available through the courtesy of Mr. Sol Stettin of the Textile Workers Union of America, AFL-CIO.

few key targets, and made extensive use of the radio to reach large audiences. In this they differed from the previous organizational techniques of the American Federation of Labor.

While no one in New Jersey became the personification of the CIO as Lewis did nationally, Carl Holderman came closest to such a position. He served as manager, regional director, and as vice-president of the Textile Workers, secretary and later president of the State CIO, and at one time as regional director of the National CIO in New Jersey.

Before the advent of the CIO, Holderman had been a manager of the New York–New Jersey District of the American Federation of Hosiery Workers. With the formation of the CIO and the Textiles Workers Organizing Committee, the Hosiery Workers joined the TWOC, CIO. Holderman, who had met and impressed Sidney Hillman of the Clothing Workers during the great textile strike of 1934, was tapped by Hillman and the TWOC to be regional director of the new organization for New Jersey in 1937.

Following his appointment, Holderman turned to the unionization of the silk and woolen mills in the Paterson-Passaic area. By mid year, 1937, Holderman was able to report that over 60 shops employing 8000 workers were under TWOC contracts, and that another 5000 workers were expected to be under contract by July, 1937. When these were brought under contract, the union won wage increases of from 10 to 50 per cent, vacations with pay, bonuses for overtime, and a reduction in the standard work week. At this time, according to Holderman, 80,000 textile workers were still unorganized in New Jersey. Because of the vigor and scale of the TWOC's organizing drives, it seems fair to say that this was the first business-like effort to unionize textile workers, in contrast to which all earlier ones were mere uprisings.

To consolidate TWOC's initial gains in the State, Holderman set up the Joint Board for New Jersey, a form of organization familiar to him from his experience with the Hosiery Workers. A joint board is like a federation of local unions, except that it has far more power over its affiliates than a federation. Initially the Joint Board comprised all textile unions in the state excepting the resuscitated Federation of Dyers and Bleachers and the Hosiery Workers. Both these groups, like the United Textile Workers, were affiliated directly with the national headquarters of TWOC. The Dyers and Bleachers Union was revived by George Baldzani of Paterson, who was its president.

At this time the Joint Board consisted of eleven local unions most of which were in the silk industry and in both major branches of weaving: broad and narrow fabrics. Broad fabrics include dress, underwear, and tie silks, and the narrow fabrics, under 24 inches in width, include woven labels, ribbons, hat bands, and braids. Workers in both plain and Jacquard weaving were therefore enrolled in the first organizational drives of the New Jersey TWOC.

The initial spurt of unionization in New Jersey's textiles lost its momentum in the face of the serious recession that set in after May, 1937. For over four years, the economic revival that began in March, 1933 and carried through to May, 1937 had been accompanied by an upsurge of unionism. With the downturn that began in the summer of 1937 and lasted for a year, the pace of unionism slowed, and in the case of the TWOC in New Jersey turned into a decline.

Unemployment became so severe that Holderman reported to the Joint Board that the textile industry in New Jersey had a 70 to 75 per cent rate of unemployment. While the Joint Board could claim 12,000 members at the end of 1937, by July, 1938 the number had been reduced to below 7500. The number of locals had increased from 11 to 17, however.

Toward the end of 1938, conditions improved, reversing the trend in membership and enabling the locals in silk to get a closed shop provision for the first time in New Jersey's textile history. (The "closed shop" requires union membership as a condition of obtaining and keeping a job.)

Improvement in economic conditions continued into 1939 and the number of locals belonging to the New Jersey State Joint Board of TWOC increased to 20. Dues-paying membership rose to 8600, still below the number attained immediately after the first organizing success of 1937.

Besides battling depressed economic conditions, it was evident that the TWOC in New Jersey was running into other roadblocks. These were stiffened employer opposition, internal dissensions, and rival organization by the AFL.

Thus, the woolen industry in the Passaic area proved to be too much at this time for the TWOC. Botany Mills, the center of the big strike of 1926, employed some 5000 workers in 1939, and was the center of the union resistance to TWOC. Other important woolen mills who likewise were able to resist TWOC were Forstmann with about 2000 employees, and Samuel Hird, with some 1500 on its payroll, and New Jersey Worsted with 500 employees.

Likewise, the Johnson & Johnson Company in New Brunswick, and American Celluloid (later the Celanese Corporation) in Newark, which the TWOC claimed were in its jurisdiction, repelled efforts by the Joint Board and its locals to organize them.

Johnson & Johnson set up company unions, succeeded later by local independent unions * that barred the way to TWOC until the war years. American Celluloid workers chose a local directly affiliated with the AFL to represent them instead of the TWOC early in 1939. In August, 1940, however the TWOC superseded the AFL at Celluloid by a vote of 523 to 491.

* A local independent union is distinguished from a company-dominated union in that it meets the National Labor Relations Board's standards enabling it to represent workers, while a company-dominated union does not.

Meanwhile, TWOC representation at two plants of Linen Thread in Paterson, won in 1937, was gradually lost to company unions, which became local independent unions by 1941. Combined these employed over 700 workers. Clark Thread, an even larger employer in Newark, resisted TWOC's early devices and remained non-union into the war period. Important carpet producers who kept out the TWOC as late as 1941 were Beattie in Little Falls and Gulbenkian in New Brunswick. On the other hand, the important Karagheusian plant in Freehold, with a thousand or more members, had joined the union early in 1940.

Within two years of its establishment in New Jersey dissension arose within the State Joint Board of the Textile Workers, CIO. It arose from both national and local sources. Nationally, part of the old United Textile Workers seceded from the TWOC, CIO, and re-joined the AFL. In New Jersey, this secession did not produce widespread or serious effects, but the rivalry did become more important later. Meanwhile in 1939, the TWOC was reconstituted as the Textile Workers Union of America, CIO.

Locally, the Joint Board of the TWUA, CIO was attacked by various local unions which disapproved of the Joint Board system. One reason for their disapproval was the cost of supporting the Board.

Another important criticism of the Joint Board stemmed from the diversity of the industrial backgrounds of the unions. For example, the carpet unions felt it more important to support associations with other locals in carpets, rather than all textile groups.

A third attack on the State Joint Board form of organization was motivated by geographic considerations. For administrative reasons locals in the various sections of the State wanted their own joint boards.

Finally, personality clashes and personal rivalries also seemed to motivate the attacks on the Joint Board. Some individuals and locals evidently wanted to cut down Holderman's power and prestige, and felt that, if the Joint Board were dissolved, his power in the state and national union would be drastically reduced. At the time of these attacks, early in 1940, the State Board had 19 written agreements with 163 employers covering over 12,000 workers. These were grouped into 23 local unions whose paying membership was under 9000.

The regional demands for decentralization were gradually met, beginning with proposals to split the state into three areas in June, 1940. The first and most important regional group was the North Jersey Joint Board. It included the counties of Passaic, Hudson, and Essex and until the Central Jersey Joint Board was organized, perhaps a year later, also Mercer, Monmouth, and Middlesex. All counties south of Mercer and Monmouth were united into a South Jersey Joint Board. Holderman, previously manager of the State Joint Board, now became manager of the North Jersey Joint Board. At this time, he also was a vice-president of the TWOC.

After Carney's death in 1940, Irving Abramson was elected President and Holderman, secretary-treasurer of the State CIO. He had been treasurer of the State CIO since 1939. Abramson was Holderman's assistant in the Textile Workers. After Abramson stepped down from the presidency in 1945, Holderman took the office. He held it until becoming the Commissioner of Labor and Industry under Governor Meyner in 1954.

THE CIO IN ELECTRICAL PRODUCTS, 1937-1940

While the Textile Workers probably led the way for the CIO in New Jersey, and was the leading CIO affiliate in the state in 1940, by virtue of numbers and leadership, the United Radio, Machine and Electrical Workers Union was a close second.

Although probably following the TWOC in terms of organizing success in New Jersey, the United Electrical, Radio and Machine Workers, CIO, soon became an important union power in the State CIO, and, in fact, by the end of World War II was the leading CIO union in New Jersey. This was an important development in State CIO affairs because the UE, as the union is familiarly known, came under the domination of the Communist Party.

The UE scored its earliest major success in New Jersey at Radio Corporation of America's Camden plant in late 1937, after a campaign that began in May, 1936. While the CIO was still within the AFL, an independent union at the RCA plant (successor to an employee representation plan) joined the United Electrical, Radio and Machine Workers and then asked management for a signed collective bargaining agreement. The company refused and a strike began. At first, 8000 of the 10,000 employed went out, but by the second week of the strike 7000 were back at work. Meanwhile, the leadership of the United Electrical Workers interested John L. Lewis in their cause and with his help, money and manpower were thrown into the campaign. Lewis himself negotiated with RCA management in New York and won an agreement to settle the issue of union representation by a National Labor Relations Board election. The election, held in August, 1936, resulted in a majority of votes cast for the UE, but the total votes cast was a minority of those eligible to vote. Nevertheless, the National Labor Relations Board ruled that the UE was the representative of the RCA workers in Camden because a company union had urged a boycott of the election. RCA at first refused to grant exclusive recognition to UE on the advice of its labor expert, General Hugh Johnson, former Administrator of the National Recovery Administration. Later (by October, 1937) his successor worked out an agreement recognizing the UE (by then part of the CIO) as the representative of all employees. Two years later the International Brotherhood of Electrical Workers, AFL, attempted to wrest the Camden plant from the UE, but lost to the UE in a NLRB election.*

* The account of the RCA plant in Camden is from Walter Galenson, *The CIO Challenge to the AFL* (Cambridge, 1960), 246, 247, 255.

Westinghouse plants making lamps in Bloomfield, Belleville, and Trenton, and the meter plant in Newark were high on the list of the UE's objectives. In 1937 company unions in these plants presented serious barriers to the UE, but by organizational drives and National Labor Relations Board elections, the UE broke through.

Likewise, seven plants making up the Edison Industries in the Oranges were organized in 1937. There the UE negotiated paid vacations and paid holidays, said to be the first for factory workers in the State.

The UE also entered the Delco-Remy plant of General Motors in Bloomfield before World War II. Prewar inroads were also made at General Electric's lamp division in Newark. In 1940, the Radio Condenser plant in Camden and the Condenser corporation in Plainfield were organized.

The "plum" of the electronics industry in New Jersey, the Kearny works of Western Electric, employing about 14,000 workers, escaped the UE, however. Its first antagonist was the Western Electric Employees Association, a local independent union. This organization, an outgrowth of a company inspired organization, barred the way to UE from 1937 to 1947. In 1947, the CIO itself took over the attempt to win the WEEA to the Telephone Workers Organizing Committee, but failed. In 1948, the International Brotherhood of Electrical Workers, AFL, stepped into the picture and succeeded in winning representation of the Western Electric plant, thus giving the AFL union the largest local unit in manufacturing in the state.

As a result of the UE's rapid gains in northern New Jersey in early 1937, the CIO, led by the UE, established the Greater Newark Industrial Union Council. Set up in September, 1937, it preceded the founding of the State CIO by just over a year. The Greater Newark IUC embraced not only Newark but all of Essex County, and Passaic, Hudson, and Union counties as well. The Newark IUC was, in fact, a forerunner of the State CIO and the county CIO councils which were later developed

from it. If the State CIO became a textile workers controlled group in 1940, the Newark Industrial Council
was, in parallel terms, a UE controlled organization
from 1937 to 1949 when the UE was ousted from the
CIO.

PETROLEUM, STEEL, AND AUTOS, 1937-1940

Except for textiles and electrical goods, the CIO
drives in other industries were either slow in starting
or, until World War II, affected smaller numbers of
workers. In petroleum refining and marketing, the CIO
Oil Workers made no headway against the major company in the state, Standard Oil of New Jersey. Standard
operated large refineries in Bayonne and Linden, but
these were represented by company and later local
independent unions. This was true, too, of tank-truck
drivers and clerical employers. Indeed, down to 1964,
the Oil Workers, and other unions, notably the Teamsters, failed to dent the independent unions in Standard
of New Jersey's installations in this state. The success
of these independents was attributed to

the willingness of Standard management to keep hands off
the new independents, plus their wage and personnel policies,
which convinced many of their employees that it would be
more advantageous to continue on an independent basis.*

The Oil Workers did make inroads in some New
Jersey locations of petroleum companies in 1937, notably
the Cities Service refinery at Linden. Previously, in 1934,
the Sinclair refineries came under union representation
as part of the national recognition extended to the Oil
Workers by Harry F. Sinclair, an action attributed to
his favorable attitude toward the New Deal.

The first Steel Workers' unit in the state appears
to have been the Worthington Pump Company (now the

* Walter Galenson, *The CIO Challenge to the AFL* (Cambridge,
1960), 416.

Worthington Company) in Harrison, organized in 1937. It was actually organized by the UE and then turned over to the Steel Workers Organizing Committee. But if the UE gave SWOC its start in New Jersey, the Steel Workers were destined to hand UE its last major setback in this state when twenty years later, in 1957, the Steel Workers wrested the Ingersoll-Rand plant in Phillipsburg from the UE.

Harrison was a center of the Steel Workers' organizing activity in the period 1937-1940. After the pump division of Worthington was unionized its meter division soon followed. The Driver-Harris Company in Harrison was won by the Steel Workers in 1937, as was the Crucible Steel plant. Crucible's Spaulding Works in Jersey City apparently came after 1937. After the war, the Jersey City operations were moved to Harrison.

National Standard, formerly Athenia Steel, in Clifton, was taken from an AFL union by the CIO Steel Workers in 1937. Roebling in Trenton and the nearby town of Roebling were won by the steel union in 1939. Overall, by 1939, the Steel Workers Organizing Committee had about 20 locals in New Jersey.

The United Auto Workers' start in New Jersey was inauspicious. At the 1937 National Convention of the UAW, no locals were represented from New Jersey. Three years later only four were present, the largest delegation coming from the General Motors plant in Linden. In addition, units at Titeflex in Newark, Hyatt Roller Bearing, and McInerney Spring and Wire each sent a delegate. A major factor in the slow start of the UAW was the factional fight between AFL and CIO supporters at national headquarters in the period 1938-1940. Although centered in Michigan, the internal UAW battling retarded the expansion of the union elsewhere. The civil war in the auto union reached a climax in 1939 with the CIO forces gaining the upper hand. The losing faction split off and set up a rival union chartered by the AFL.

In New Jersey, as elsewhere, the rival auto unions

clashed with more victories won by the UAW-CIO. In a key contest at General Motor's Linden plant in April, 1940, the UAW-CIO overwhelmed the AFL auto union in a National Labor Relations Board election, 2,135 votes to 65, with 285 going to neither.

A few months later, in August, 1940, the UAW-CIO won the Bloomfield Warehouse of the General Motors Sales Corporation in another National Labor Relations Board poll. The following year the UAW gained representation rights after another Board election at the Air Associates plant in Bendix. Brewster Aeronautical in Newark was apparently organized before America entered World War II. However, the real upsurge of the UAW in New Jersey, like that of so many other unions, came with World War II.

During the height of the prewar CIO organizing drives, the Auto and the Rubber Workers had begun to use the sit-down strike with devastating impact in Michigan and Ohio. Governor Harold G. Hoffman, eyeing the organizing activities at the Thermoid Company in Trenton in the early months of 1937, warned the Rubber Workers Organizing Committee and the CIO in general against using the sit-down strike in New Jersey. He declared that

a labor union has no more right to take possession of a factory than a band of gangsters has to take possession of a bank, and when to such unlawful taking of possession there is added the theft and destruction of property, and the use of threat of violence and armed resistance to government authority, there is no difference between the two either in principle or degree.*

In the spring of 1937 the Thermoid Company was struck (but not with a sit-down) and Governor Hoffman sent in the State Police. These were soon withdrawn, but this action earned the Governor the title of strikebreaker. In addition, the inflammatory nature of his

* *New York Times,* Feb. 16, 1937.

remarks on strikes embroiled him in disputes with groups like the League of Women Voters, as well as labor.

THE STATE FEDERATION OF LABOR, 1933-1940

A changeover in the leadership of the Federation in 1934 brought Louis P. Marciante to the presidency, a post he held until his death in 1961. Since Vincent Murphy defeated Hugh Reilly for secretary-treasurer of the Federation in 1932, the Federation had an entirely new administration at a crucial turning point in labor history, the advent of the New Deal. Together, Marciante and Murphy guided the State Federation for the next quarter-century and longer.

Despite their inadequate coverage, the figures in Appendix C support the conclusion that affiliates of the New Jersey Federation grew slowly during the New Deal years, 1933-1939. It was only with the outbreak of war in Europe that the State AFL made more rapid gains.

One of the most difficult membership problems besetting the Federation throughout its history and a major reason for the difficulty of gauging its size and growth was the failure of many eligible unions in New Jersey to join the State AFL organization. A survey in 1935 showed that of 966 eligible unions known in the state less than half, 418, belonged to the New Jersey Federation of Labor.*

The slow recovery of the AFL unions, especially those in building was due to the high unemployment in construction throughout the period, 1933-1940. Under these conditions, unions discouraged new entrants to the trades while so many members were out of work. Moreover, much public construction at this time was undertaken by the Works Progress Administration and the Public Works Administration. Although these agencies paid prevailing wages, the workers were not officially counted

* New Jersey State Federation of Labor, *Proceedings of Convention, 1935*, 30.

as employed, nor did they belong to bargaining units represented by unions. Hence, they did not add to the rolls of union membership.

The 1935 Convention of the State Federation took note of the dissension in the National AFL over craft versus industrial unionism. A majority report on the issue echoing the national AFL position called upon the dissident Committee for Industrial Organization to conduct its program within the framework of the AFL. A minority report called upon the Executive Council of the AFL to rescind its order suspending the unions of the CIO from the American Federation of Labor and to refer the issue to the next convention. The New Jersey Federation Convention rejected the minority report and adopted the majority report.

The split between AFL and CIO in New Jersey was completed at the 1937 Convention of the State Federation when, at the behest of William Green, President of the AFL, it barred all New Jersey CIO unions from taking seats at the convention. Next, the New Jersey State Federation voted to expel all organizations affiliated with the Committee for Industrial Organization with only one dissent among the 600 delegates. The dissenter, David Herman of the Cafeteria Workers Union of Newark, also attacked the Convention's endorsement of United States Senator A. Harry Moore as "a horse trading convention for Frank Hague, Mayor of Jersey City." * After the convention, the Essex County Central Labor Union met to consider expelling Mr. Herman for embarrassing the convention.

President Marciante attacked the CIO for using "the despicable bribe to have local officers vote their membership into the CIO without taking the trouble to give local union members the right to vote on the question." Marciante labeled as a "dastardly lie" the charge that the AFL did not care to organize the unskilled. Despite this allegation, the AFL had few unskilled workers in its ranks in 1937.

* *New York Times,* Sept. 14 and Sept. 16, 1937.

Further AFL reaction to the CIO in New Jersey came at a meeting in Newark on December 4, 1937, attended by 50 state AFL leaders. Their plans included the establishment of a central office and the formation of "militant" organizing committees, apparently to resemble those of the CIO.

Nearly a year later William Green took note of the State Federation's support against the CIO in much the same vein as his predecessor, Samuel Gompers, who had praised the New Jersey Federation of Trades and Labor Unions in 1890 for combating the Knights of Labor. Thus Green told the 1938 convention of the New Jersey Federation, "I am proud of you, proud of the New Jersey State Federation of Labor. Why? Because under the most trying circumstances in season and out of season, day in and day out it has proven its loyalty and devotion to the philosophy and principles of the AFL." * To the CIO, Green declared there would be no surrender to dualism, to secessionism, or rival movements.

While the general upturn in the New Jersey Federation's membership was slow from 1933 to 1939, some groups, notably the Teamsters and the Hotel, Restaurant Employees and Bartenders Union, appear to have moved ahead rapidly. The end of Prohibition helped to stimulate the growth of the Teamsters among brewery workers and drivers in Newark, while the Hotel and Bartenders Union gained from the re-opening of bars.

In addition, new inroads were made by AFL unions among government employees. Thus, in 1938, with Newark under a pro-labor administration, the municipal workers were organized. Gains by locals of the Amalgamated Meat Cutters and Butcher Workmen, and the Retail Clerks led local units of these unions to join the State Federation in 1940.

---

* New Jersey State Federation of Labor, *Proceedings of Convention, 1938,* 247-248.

The principal unions not affiliated with the AFL nationally and in New Jersey at the beginning of the New Deal were the unions of operating employees on the railways, notably the Locomotive Engineers, the Locomotive Firemen and Enginemen, the Railroad Trainmen, and the Railway Conductors. However, under the impact of Section 7 (a) of the National Industrial Recovery Act (1933), and the National Labor Relations Act (1935) many unaffiliated local labor organizations sprang up in New Jersey. In fact, New Jersey was among the leading states in this type of organization.

Initially, most of these organizations were inspired and controlled by employers. Many were abolished by order of the National Labor Relations Board, some were won over by bona fide unions, and still others were reconstituted so as to meet the requirements of the law.

In New Jersey, the last group, the local independent unions, was particularly strong in petroleum, in telephones, and in a variety of manufacturing industries.

Like Standard of New Jersey, the American Telephone and Telegraph Company had set up employee representation plans. Some of these dated back to World War I or shortly thereafter. Others were organized by the company during the early years of the New Deal. After validation of the Wagner Act in 1937, however, the company gradually relinquished its grip on these organizations. In the Bell Telephone Company of New Jersey, there were organizations among operators, accounting, plant, and other departments. Western Electric, another subsidiary of A T & T also had an employee representation plan at Kearney which evolved into a local independent union, as already noted in our account of the United Electrical, Radio and Machine Workers, CIO.

Beginning in 1938, the independents in the Bell systems and Western Electric throughout the country joined in a loose association known as the National Federation of Telephone Unions. A leading figure in the

NFTU was a representative from the Western Electric Employees Association, Joseph Beirne, who grew up and went to school in Jersey City. Beirne became president of the National Federation of Telephone Unions in 1943.

The New Jersey Bell unions and the Kearny Western Electric Employees Association joined the NFTU, but since the association was loose, their affiliation, especially that of the WEEA, was tenuous. To remedy this chronic weakness of the association, the NFTU re-organized itself as the Communications Workers of America in 1947, but two important unions in New Jersey apparently remained aloof. These were the WEEA, and the Telephone Workers of New Jersey (representing plant workers and installers). Eventually both joined the International Brotherhood of Electrical Workers, AFL. In 1949 Joseph Beirne led the Communications Workers of America into the CIO.

MEMBERSHIP AND EXTENT OF ORGANIZATION, 1939

Based on the only state data extant,* total union membership in 1939 in New Jersey stood at 200,000 (Table 8). Of this number, 123,000 were in AFL unions, 44,000 in CIO affiliates, and 33,000 in unaffiliated unions. The margin of AFL numerical strength in New Jersey was even greater than it was nationally in 1939. Thus, while the AFL outnumbered the CIO in the country 1.6 to 1 in 1939, in New Jersey the AFL's margin in the same year was 2.8 to 1. The count of the independent unions' membership is the least satisfactory because of the difficulty of obtaining data on the local independents.

Relative to the State's non-agricultural employment in 1939, the extent of organization stood at 16 per cent, a figure well below the average of 23.5 per cent for the Middle Atlantic Region (which comprises New York, New Jersey, and Pennsylvania), and the national average of 21.5 per cent.

* Leo Troy, *Distribution of Union Membership Among the States, 1939 and 1953* (New York, 1957).

TABLE 8

UNION MEMBERSHIP IN NEW JERSEY, NEW YORK, PENNSLYVANIA,
AND THE UNITED STATES, 1939 AND 1953 *

	New Jersey	New York	Pennsyl- vania	Middle Atlantic Region	United States
		(In thousands)			
1939					
AFL	122.8	531.6	251.3	905.7	3,851.2
CIO	44.3	255.0	424.2	723.5	1,796.9
Unaffiliated	33.5	173.2	63.4	269.8	869.6
Total	200.6	959.8	738.6	1,899.0	6,517.7
1953					
AFL	397.8	1,378.4	717.2	2,493.4	9,972.0
CIO	201.6	529.4	536.0	1,267.0	4,560.4
Unaffiliated	46.0	144.0	287.5	477.5	1,684.9
Total	645.4	2,051.8	1,540.7	4,237.9	16,217.3
Percentage of increase	221.7%	113.8%	108.6%	123.2%	148.8%

* Leo Troy, "Union Membership in New Jersey," *Review of New Jersey Business*, July, 1956 XII, 6.

Clearly, therefore, the New Deal did not bring the great gains in union strength to New Jersey as it did nationally or in other states. As we have seen, the CIO's growth was largely limited to two unions, the Textile Workers and the United Electrical Workers; and most affiliates of the State Federation grew slowly from 1933 to 1940.

Actually, the lag of unionism in New Jersey as of 1939 was even greater than the foregoing suggests. By assuming that this state's industries were as organized as their national counterparts in 1939, we were able to create hypothetical figures of what New Jersey's union population ought to have been. On this basis, the actual fell below the expected by nearly 60,000. Hence, union population of this state lagged behind other major industrial states in 1939.

The first years of the war did not bring gains in employment and membership to the organized sections of New Jersey's textiles, notably carpets and silks. The shortage of materials actually reduced employment and union numbers by 1942.

Late in the following year, however, the Textile Workers, CIO, made historic break-throughs in wool in Passaic and in the Johnson & Johnson Company in New Brunswick and vicinity. In December, 1943, the TWUA won the most important wool manufacturer, Botany Worsted mills, employing some 4000 workers. The victory was followed by organization of Forstmann, and New Jersey Worsted. The gains in the wool industry of Passaic County were so great that the North Jersey Joint Board was subdivided into county joint boards for Passaic, Hudson, and Essex.

Early in 1944, after seven years of organizing efforts, the Textile Workers defeated the independent unions in Johnson & Johnson by means of government-held elections.

The United Electrical, Radio and Machine Workers made exceptionally rapid gains during the war years. It won National Labor Relations Board elections at Westinghouse Meter in Newark, Tung-Sol also in Newark, Phelps-Dodge in Elizabeth, and Singer Sewing in Elizabethport. Compared to its 7200 members in 1939, by the end of the war the UE probably had 40,000 members in New Jersey.

Equally impressive were the inroads made by the United Auto Workers, CIO in Ford Motor, Mack Truck, and in the aircraft plants of Bendix, Wright, Curtiss, and Brewster. The upsurge of employment in these and the General Motors works already represented by the UAW pushed the union to record numbers of members.

Similarly, the Steel Workers expanded tremendously on its small prewar base in the metal fabricating industry of the state.

Overall, the CIO membership advanced very rapidly in New Jersey. Figures of membership of the State Industrial Council, although more inclusive than the comparable ones for the State AFL, did not include all CIO unions, showed a growth from 53,000 in 1941 to 152,000 in 1945 (Appendix D). During the war years, the State Industrial Union Council claimed between three and four hundred thousand members in CIO unions.

Unions belonging to the AFL likewise joined the wartime expansion of unionism. The growth of military installations at Fort Dix and Camp Kilmer boosted the building trades unions, who now made marked gains. The Machinists, who competed with the UAW for members in the aircraft industry, and the Teamsters also increased in New Jersey during the war years. Membership in the New Jersey State Federation which stood at about fifty-two thousand in 1940 climbed to about eighty-seven thousand in 1945 (Appendix C).

Both the Federation and the Industrial Union Council gave full support to the war effort, backing the no-strike pledge. However, the Federation backed AFL President Green's attack on Roosevelt's "hold the line" on wages and on the "job freeze." Affiliates of both showed good records in contributing to the war effort, not only in preventing strikes but in encouraging members to buy war bonds.

THE COMMUNIST PARTY AND THE STATE CIO

Like the CIO nationally, the State Industrial Union Council from its origin in 1938 until about 1947 was torn between Communist and non-Communist factions. John L. Lewis banned Communists from the United Mine Workers, but not from the CIO. Apparently, their effectiveness in organizing outweighed their political liability to the CIO.

However, splits between the CIO and the Communists soon developed, and, typically, these arose from wide differences on foreign and domestic affairs rather than trade union matters. The first important break came in 1939 when the Communists, then in a "neutralist" phase opposing military preparation, came out against President Roosevelt's proposal for peacetime conscription. Isolationists who also opposed the proposal were therefore supported by the Communist Party.

Consequently, since John L. Lewis was an isolationist and against conscription, William Carney, a Lewis protégé in New Jersey and President of the State CIO since 1938, also came out against conscription. Supporting him in the State CIO were the United Electrical, Radio and Machine Workers, the center of the Party's strength in the CIO, and the Secretary of the State organization, Leonard Goldsmith, an alleged party-liner or member.

Carney and Goldsmith teamed up again in 1940 to oppose the re-nomination and re-election of Roosevelt, each adopting his course for his own reasons: Lewis opposed Roosevelt (for several reasons), so Carney opposed him because his mentor did. Goldsmith opposed Roosevelt in accordance with the Communist Party line. Carney died before his opposition might have provoked a fight against him, but Goldsmith was nearly expelled from office because of his position. When the Sate CIO convened and chose a successor to Carney, Irving Abramson of the Textile Workers, the IUC replaced Goldsmith with Carl Holderman.

Germany's attack on Russia changed the Party line from opposition to the war to full cooperation. Thus, the major differences in domestic and foreign matters were submerged between 1941 and 1945.

Nevertheless, cleavages showed up in the State CIO with the UE criticizing the reformist Democrat, Governor Charles Edison, who was backed by the rest of the CIO. Likewise, the UE, through its control of the Hudson County Industrial Union Council, supported the CIO's bitter opponent, Mayor Frank Hague, in his bid to get Senator A. Harry Moore the Democratic Party's nomination for governor in 1943.

When World War II ended and the Cold War began,

the split between the CIO and the Communists re-opened and became unbridgeable.

Beginning in 1946 at the Ninth Convention, the State IUC officially condemned the Communist Party. Of the eight county and city councils in the State in 1946, only the Greater Newark Industrial Union Council, which was controlled by the UE, opposed the vote. (When the UE was expelled from the CIO in 1949, the Newark Council was replaced by the Essex-West Hudson Industrial Union Council.) In the same year a group of CIO unionists formed the New Jersey Committee for Democratic Trade Unionism to war upon the Communist Party within the movement. Holderman, a long-time foe of the CP, disapproved of the Committee because it might divide the opponents of the Party.

At the next convention, the United Electrical, Radio and Machine Workers withdrew from the State CIO when its choice of representatives to the State IUC were brushed aside by the convention in favor of other UE leaders. Afterwards, the convention recorded its support of the Marshall Plan, a measure opposed by the Communist Party and the UE.

As a result of the continuing purge of Party-dominated locals, the State Industrial Union Council broke the power of the Party in the state organization by the end of 1948. At that time only 56 of over 525 locals affiliated were still said to be under CP control. While not ex-pelled, the CP unions began withholding payment of per capita dues, which violated the CIO Constitution, and, of course, reduced the State IUC's income. A special convention was called to raise the per capita dues which it did, from 3 to 4 per cent per month. The announced loss of membership due to the walk-out of the Communist-dominated unions was thirty thousand.

The attack on the Communist Party soon divided the membership of the affected unions. UE, with a state membership of about 42,000 in 1947-1948, was reported to be split with 14 locals and 17,000 members for the CIO leadership, and 22 locals representing 25,000 members still accepting the leadership of the UE. The fissures continued to widen, as when UE Local 103 ordered its officers to sign the non-Communist oaths required by the Taft-Hartley Act as a condition of using the NLRB's process of conducting elections and restraining unfair labor practices. It was the policy of the national UE at this time not to comply. It should be noted that some well known non-Communists, notably John L. Lewis, also refused to sign, branding the requirement as degrading and inequitable. The provision was finally dropped from the law.

By the time the national CIO began expelling unions for accepting Communist leadership in 1949-1950, the New Jersey IUC had already overcome the Party. The New Jersey State IUC therefore anticipated its parent body by some two years in destroying the CP within the union movement.

The national CIO expulsions led to the chartering of new unions and drives by existing ones to recapture the expelled membership. In New Jersey, the newly-chartered International Union of Electrical Radio and Machine Workers was especially important. With the help of the State IUC it captured most of the UE's membership here. In general, CIO unions regained the membership of Communist-led unions, and AFL attempts to capitalize on the situation were surprisingly unsuccessful. The most significant raid in New Jersey by an AFL affiliate, the Boilermakers, took a 3000-member local of the Marine and Shipbuilding Workers, a union which stayed with the CIO after purging itself of some CP followers.

Offsetting some of the losses from expulsion and raids by AFL unions, the CIO picked up strength from the affiliation of the Communications Workers of America in 1949, as previously noted. As part of the affiliation arrangement between the CWA and the CIO, the Telephone Workers Organizing Committee, CIO was merged with the new affiliate.

The postwar economic readjustments led to a number of protracted strikes in autos, steel, and electrical manufacturing. In New Jersey, one of the largest post-World War II strikes occurred between the United Electrical, Radio and Machine Workers and the Singer Sewing Company, at the company's Elizabethport plant. The strike lasted from April 21, 1949 to October 17, 1949, and involved about seven thousand workers.

It arose over work standards used in the piece-system of wage payments, a demand for general wage increase, work schedules, and a widespread belief that the UE's aggressive stand was in furtherance of Communist policies. A study of the strike dismissed the last as a real issue and singled out the first as the basic cause of the strike.* It should be noted, in passing, that the UE was purged from the CIO in New Jersey about two years before the strike, and was expelled from the national CIO later in 1949.

The strike was free of violence, one of the reasons being the good job the UE did in providing for the minimal needs of the strikers. All members of District 4 of UE of which the Elizabethport Local was a part, contributed 25 cents a week to a relief fund which totalled about $15,000 a week. Each striker received $5.50 a week and an additional $1.50 weekly allowance for each dependent. The Debs branch of the Socialist Party in Elizabeth supplied gifts of food and clothing to the strikers despite the basic differences between Socialists and the Communist leadership of the national UE. The National Farmer's Union, Eastern Division, donated food weekly beginning in June, 1949. The first shipment consisted of a ton and a half of eggs, live chickens, fresh and canned vegetables. Local merchants provided re-

* Kenneth L. Biro, "An Analysis of the Singer Strike, Elizabethport, New Jersey, 1949" (Masters thesis, Rutgers University, 1950), 85-86.

frigerator space, and a poultry market contributed free slaughtering and dressing.

The estimated loss in wages during the strike was $12,000,000; sales losses were put at $20,000,000. Local merchants suffered severely, a few being forced out of business.

Insofar as the issues were concerned, little was changed: "The contract terms were similar to those embodied in previous contracts." *

The successor to the UE, after its expulsion from the CIO, the International Union of Electrical Workers, was involved in another strike of even greater magnitude, from October 15, 1955, to March 20, 1956.

It was part of a national walk-out against Westinghouse, which in New Jersey involved over 7000 workers at plants in Newark, Jersey City, Trenton, Metuchen, Bloomfield, and Belleville. On October 24, the United Electrical Workers, now unaffiliated, joined the nation-wide strike against Westinghouse, adding another 1000 workers in New Jersey to the strike list.

As in the UE's 1949 strike at Singer in Elizabethport, the main issue was work standards. Wage increases along with employment security and fringe benefits were also involved. However, unlike the Singer stoppage, this strike was marked with violence. On December 16, 1955, strikers at Bloomfield and Trenton turned away cars seeking to enter the plant, to preclude any return-to-work movement, and in several instances threw rocks at the automobiles. Westinghouse then succeeded in obtaining injunctions to halt mass picketing. Violence broke out again in Bloomfield when two policemen trying to escort cars through the picket lines were struck by a car sending both to the hospital. Four others were injured, although not seriously.

The resentment of the workers may be gauged from

* Kenneth L. Biro, "An Analysis of the Singer Strike, Elizabethport, New Jersey, 1949" (Masters thesis, Rutgers University, 1950), 57.

the fact that at Christmas, a company offer to make interest-free loans to employees was accepted by only 800 workers in New Jersey. The union took a neutral stand on the loan offer.

Local government tried to help resolve the strike when 13 mayors from affected cities including Mayors Leo P. Carlin of Newark, Bernard J. Berry of Jersey City, and Donald H. Scott of Bloomfield, went to Pittsburgh in January to try to bring about a settlement. On the day the mayors met with management and union leaders, another union with agreements in Westinghouse, the International Brotherhood of Electrical Workers, AFL, signed new contracts with the company. Nevertheless, the strike by the IUE, CIO, and the UE, independent, continued for two months longer.

The final settlement resulted in minor gains over the company's offer of some five and one-half months earlier. The cost to the workers and company were staggering. New Jersey workers were estimated to have lost over $18,000,000, while the company's total loss in sales was put at $290,000,000.

ORGANIZATION, 1945-1964

Generally, the unions in New Jersey made continuing if slower advances in organizing from 1945 to 1950. However, the Korean War, like all previous conflicts, increased employment and thus membership in unionized plants. As a result, New Jersey, which had been below the national average in the proportion of non-farm workers organized in 1939, exceeded it in 1953. Whereas the national average of non-farm workers organized was 32.6 per cent in 1953, New Jersey's was 35.2 per cent. In the rankings of states, New Jersey moved from twenty-third place in 1939 to fourteenth in 1953.

Unionism's rapid growth from the beginning of World War II to the end of the Korean War lifted its 1953 membership of 645,400 (Table 8) above that "expected" on the basis of its industrial make-up. It would thus appear that the lag which existed in 1939 had been made up. But had it?

Actually, since the "expected" figures depend on national concepts which include states low in organization like those in the South, it can be shown that New Jersey still lagged in union growth when compared to other industrial states of the North, Midwest, and Far West.

From 1953 to 1964 membership in New Jersey declined about five per cent or half as rapidly as did union membership throughout the nation.

AFL-CIO MERGER

The AFL and CIO merged nationally in December, 1955, but in New Jersey the two federations did not join until September, 1961, nearly six years later. New Jersey, in fact, was the last state in which merger was achieved. Following the national merger of the AFL and CIO, the new federation prohibited either state group from holding conventions to elect officers or change their constitutions.

Nationally, the basis of the merger was mutual recognition of the bargaining units represented rather than exclusive jurisdiction, the issue on which the two wings of organized labor had broken apart. The two federations agreed on a no-raiding pact in 1953, and this did reduce inter-union attacks. In addition, the passing of two leaders, William Green and Philip Murray, both identified with the split, and their replacement by George Meany and Walter Reuther, both younger and more anxious for reconciliation, contributed to the consummation of the merger at the national level. Ironically, the two top New Jersey leaders and opponents on each side, like the two leading national antagonists, also died before the merger: Holderman died in 1959, and Marciante in 1961.

Locally, the philosophical gulf between the two federations was wider than it was nationally, and the

AFL-CIO Merger in New Jersey, 1961
Courtesy of Newark News, September 25, 1961

mutual distrust, if not dislike, of the leadership ran more deeply than it did on the national level.

From the AFL standpoint, the trade unionism of the CIO was suspect. It involved many workers who had little skill and whose attachment to the union was determined by employment. In contrast, the craft union member usually retained his membership even when he was unemployed in order to maintain his rights to the union's death, sickness, or disability funds. There were also important differences in organizational structure. Thus, while the locus of power in AFL unions is at the local level, often in the hands of a local's executive board, the CIO's structural arrangements put the power in the regional office of the national or international union. Under this system, it is alleged that state and local representatives have far less local authority in contrast with AFL leaders.

Politically, the AFL regarded the CIO leadership to be radical and, in some instances, under Communist influence. President Marciante long made it a cardinal principle that no merger between the AFL and CIO was possible until the CIO had been purged of Communists. Marciante's anti-communism was so intense that he once personally supervised the expulsion of a man distributing the *Daily Worker* at a State Federation convention. However, despite the fact that the New Jersey CIO was one of the first state organizations to purge itself of the Communist Party's influence, the merger of the state organizations was the last in the country.

To the CIO, the AFL was conservative and without adequate sympathy for the factory worker. They were the "labor aristocracy" who all too easily "ennobled" corrupt labor leaders like Joe Fay. The AFL's political alliance with Mayor Hague of Jersey City, no practitioner of democracy, hardly suggested a concern for the workers in the eyes of the CIO. Marciante had long been a friend of Hague and said of the AFL's relation with the Mayor that "no AFL labor leader was restricted in Jersey City" * in contrast to CIO leaders, especially in the late 1930's). Actually, Marciante was wrong since Hague had shackled the AFL in Jersey City for most of the decade of the thirties.

Because of the stalemate in merging, the national AFL-CIO announced in February, 1960 that after four years of efforts to bring about a voluntary merger, "it will give its warring factions in New Jersey six weeks to work out a state-wide merger or face a shot-gun wedding." ** About six weeks later, in March, 1960, George Meany, President of the AFL-CIO, issued orders for a forced merger, the second since he applied pressure in Michigan in 1958. President Marciante approved this approach, declaring that "this is what we have been urging a number of years on the basis that a voluntary merger was impossible." †

Meany sent aides to New Jersey to bring about the forced merger convention. However, in May, 1960, a special CIO convention numbering over one thousand delegates almost unanimously rejected Meany's plans for amalgamation. Under Meany's merger plans, the AFL would have gotten two of the three top posts. All other jobs in each organization would be guaranteed. Representation on the executive board was to be based on membership.

Sol Stetin, speaking for the CIO said that his organization wanted "equality not equity" in the merger, and expressed fear that AFL control would not only mean the end of the CIO group, but that its policies, program, and militancy would suffer at the hands of the AFL's leadership.‡

The CIO then announced it would boycott the merger convention called by Meany's two aides, especially in the face of the AFL's declaration that it intended to nominate candidates for all officers in the merged convention.

* *Newark News,* March 31, 1961.
** *New York Times,* Feb. 9, 1960.
† *New York Times,* Feb. 9, 1960.
‡ *New York Times,* May 8, 1960.

Since the AFL outnumbered the CIO, this would have eliminated all CIO influence in the operation of the new federation.

As a result of the wrangle over the sharing of top jobs, Meany's aides canceled the proposed merger convention a few hours before it was to begin, and returned to Washington to confer with President Meany on methods of breaking the impasse.

Meanwhile, an internal struggle over the presidency of the CIO in 1960 further complicated the merger. A contest between Paul Krebs and Joel Jacobson, both "heirs" of Carl Holderman, ended with the election of Jacobson. After Holderman went to Trenton as Commissioner of Labor and Industry in 1954, Krebs succeeded him as president and held the job until displaced in 1960. The United Automobile Workers, Krebs' organization, walked out of the convention, and about 48 locals voted to petition the UAW's executive board to approve withdrawal from the state and county CIO councils. However, the Auto Workers stayed in the CIO.

The AFL also opposed Jacobson, and initially wished to deny him any top post in the new organizations. However, despite their desire to control all top jobs in the new AFL-CIO, the final merger agreement September 25, 1961, provided for two executive vice-presidents from the CIO, one of which was filled by Jacobson.

A few months before the merger Louis P. Marciante, President of the State AFL since 1934, died. Although he had had very little formal education, he had risen to the presidency of the State Federation. He was a member of the International Brotherhood of Electrical Workers, an organization which he joined as an apprentice in 1915 when he was sixteen years of age. Two years later he became a business agent, but then joined the Marines. After his military service, he rejoined the union movement to become secretary of the Mercer County Building Trades Council. In 1932 he became a member of the Executive Board of the State Federation. The following year he was elected president of the County Central Trades Union and was named by President Roosevelt to the Regional Labor Board administering Section 7 (a) of the National Industrial Recovery Act. He defeated Thomas Eames to become president of the State Federation in 1934.

Two weeks after Marciante's death on March 30, 1961, the Executive Board of the State Federation chose Vincent J. Murphy as president of the Federation. Thus, under the merger agreement which gave the presidency to the AFL, Murphy became the first president of the New Jersey State AFL-CIO. The agreement also gave the job of secretary-treasurer to the AFL, and Charles Marciante, son of the late president, was named to this post. Jacobson became the first executive vice-president and Victor Leonardis, former secretary-treasurer of the State IUC, the second executive vice-president. All were to hold office until the 1964 Convention, after which selections would be "in accordance with the Constitution, without regard to previous affiliation." * The Executive Board was to consist of 25 vice-presidents from the State AFL, 12 from the CIO, and 2 more to be chosen by the Board of the merged organization. Membership of the merged federation, based on per capita receipts was 391,600 in 1962 and 438,900 in 1963. No estimate is available for 1961, the year of the merger.

In the Convention of 1964, the two offices of executive vice-presidents, both held by former CIO men were abolished. Thereupon, the CIO group, or most of it, withdrew and a few days later held the first convention of the New Jersey State Industrial Union Council, AFL-CIO, thus re-establishing the break between the old AFL and CIO in fact if not in name.

* Merger Agreement Between the New Jersey State Federation of Labor and the New Jersey Industrial Union Council, 1961, p. 2.

CIO 'walks out' in union split

Joel Jacobson

Delegates listen to speakers at AFL-CIO convention

Vincent J. Murphy

New Jersey AFL-CIO Split, June 1964
Courtesy of the Newark Star Ledger, June 16, 1964

Most CIO unions, if not all ceased or were expected to cease making any affiliation payments to the AFL-CIO.

At the inception of the New Deal, the fortunes of organized labor in New Jersey were at ebb tide. However, from 1933 to the outbreak of World War II, continuing gains in organizing workers were made, especially by the newly formed unions of the Congress of Industrial Organizations. The CIO sprang from a cleavage in the AFL that began in 1935 and lasted nationally for twenty years. In New Jersey, the split was not bridged until 1961—and then was opened again in 1964.

The war years gave a tremendous impetus to union growth. After the war, a series of strikes disrupted the industrial life of the state and nation, one of the most notable occurring at the Singer plant at Elizabethport in 1949. Six years later, an even bigger strike of Westinghouse workers took place.

Internally, the CIO faced the problem of Communist domination of some leading affiliates. The New Jersey State CIO was one of the first to act against the Communists, anticipating the national CIO's expulsion of eleven Communist-dominated unions by two years.

The great gains made by New Jersey unions between 1939 and 1953 made the state one of the most highly organized in the nation. Compared to 1953, the union population of the state in 1964 has declined, paralleling the general decline in the nation.

Early in 1965, the split within the New Jersey State AFL-CIO was nominally healed, as a result of a plan worked out by George Meany, President of the National AFL-CIO. As of April 1, 1965, the two executive posts held by the CIO in the state organization and eliminated by the numerically superior AFL wing in June 1964 were restored along with the original salaries of $14,000 a year. However, the former officeholders, Joel

R. Jacobson and Victor D. Leonardis did not return to the restored positions. Appointed in their places were Richard A. Lynch of local 410 of the International Union of Electrical, Radio and Machine Workers in Bloomfield, and John Georges of local 1668 of the United Automobile Workers in East Newark.

Local unions affiliated with the old CIO rejoined the State AFL-CIO on April 1, 1965, but the New Jersey State Industrial Union Council, set-up in June, 1964 continues to function and be led by Jacobson and Leonardis. In a joint statement they described the role of the State IUC to be one of "formulating and presenting a militant labor program in the interests of industrial workers throughout New Jersey." *

The present arrangement indicates that the attempted power-play of the AFL wing to push the CIO unions into the background of the State AFL-CIO had been thwarted by the opposition of George Meany. His intervention compelled the State AFL group to reestablish the two offices they claimed to have legally abolished by convention action in June 1964. However, the State AFL leaders were not compelled to accept the return of their old antagonists, Jacobson and Leonardis. Meanwhile, the CIO group retains its separate organization, program and leadership, and can be expected to pursue different actions in politics than the AFL-CIO which will remain under the control of the AFL.

* *New York Times,* March 17, 1965.

VI

LAW AND LABOR RELATIONS

Aᴌᴛʜᴏᴜɢʜ ᴛʀᴀᴅᴇ ᴜɴɪᴏɴꜱ were able to organize skilled workmen with very little government intervention on behalf of labor, they were unable to make important and lasting inroads among the great masses of factory workers until 1935, when Congress, in the Wagner Act, protected their right to organize and bargain collectively. It would be fair to state therefore, that much of the present power and status of trade unions is owed to governmental regulation of labor relations.

In this chapter we shall examine briefly the historical process which changed the status of unions from an illegal to a protected institution under the law, and how the government, after using its enormous power to foster unionism, increased its intervention to regulate the internal activities of unions in the interest of individual members. Finally, we shall review the work of state agencies that have sought to prevent disputes or to resolve them once they have begun.

Cᴏɴꜱᴘɪʀᴀᴄʏ Dᴏᴄᴛʀɪɴᴇ

Throughout much of the nineteenth century, labor policy in New Jersey, as in the other states, was chiefly made by the state judicial system and police courts. English common law not at variance with the state or federal constitutions, and as modified by statutes, was applied to the labor market. Of overriding importance in employer-employeee relations was the common law governing master and servant. Under common law, combinations of workers having economic objectives such as raising wages were indictable for criminal conspiracy.

Thus, in the period from 1806 to 1842, in 17 landmark cases, unions were held to be illegal under the common-law doctrine of conspiracy. As a result, many tried to cloak their economic actions in language which might deflect charges of conspiracy. Thus, a union of leather workers in Newark during a dispute with their employers in 1835 declared as their motto, "United to support but not combined to injure." Perhaps by such devices, but more likely because employers were reluctant to carry their labor disputes to court, there are no known cases of conspiracy involving unions in New Jersey during the years 1806 to 1842 when the doctrine was most prominent. Indeed, it was only after the doctrine was abandoned in most leading industrial states of the country, after the *Commonwealth of Massachusetts* v. *Hunt* case in 1842, that unions in New Jersey ran afoul of the conspiracy doctrine. As a result of that decision, unions as economic organizations attempting to maintain or improve their members' living standards became legal in Massachusetts and numerous states which followed her lead.

Nevertheless, the conspiracy doctrine continued to linger in some states by statute and one of these was New Jersey. Thus, in the *Donaldson* case in 1867, the Supreme Court of New Jersey re-affirmed the trade unions' position under the common law of conspiracy. The remarkable feature of this case was that the court did not apply the New Jersey statute on conspiracy, but the common-law version which Massachusetts had dropped twenty-five years before. The Court ruled that although the union combination was not in restraint of trade, and not subject to the New Jersey statute, as the State argued, it found that common law was not superseded by the statute and, therefore if the facts warranted, the case could be tried on the common-law doctrine itself. * And the Court did find that the facts (refusal to work with non-union employees) constituted an illegal conspiracy at common law. It agreed that the union in this case, as in the landmark *Hunt* case, sought a closed shop, but while the Massachusetts Court ruled it a legal objective," the object of the combination in the case before this court, was to occasion a *particular* result which was mischievous, and by means which were oppressive." **

Thus, unions as economic institutions remained outside the sanction of New Jersey law. Although this position was more often ignored than not, since, as we have seen, some unions had a continuous existence from 1834 to 1887, and engaged in strikes while legally this action was in doubt, nevertheless the threat of the conspiracy doctrine probably deterred union growth and activities in New Jersey. It is noteworthy that one of the goals of the New Jersey State Labor Congress was to change the trade union's status under the law of conspiracy.

In 1883, the efforts of the Congress, and its successor organization, the Federation of Organized Trades and Labor Unions, were successful and the legislature abolished the conspiracy doctrine as applied to unions. Eleven years later, the state legislature abolished another obstacle to unionism when it outlawed "yellow-dog" contracts. (A yellow-dog contract is an employee's promise not to join or remain a member of a union as a condition of employment. It is the opposite of the closed shop.)

LEGAL RIGHT TO ORGANIZE

The pendulum went completely to the other side of the legal spectrum: organizing for collective bargaining, once illegal under the conspiracy doctrine as applied by most state and municipal courts, became protected

* *State* v. *Donaldson* (1867), 32 *New Jersey Law Reports*, 151.
** *State* v. *Donaldson* (1867), *New Jersey Law Reports*, 151, at 158. Emphasis added.

activity under federal and later New Jersey law. The right to join a union, to bargain collectively, and to engage in concerted activities for purposes of collective bargaining or other mutual aid or protection became legally protected, first by the Railway Labor Act of 1926 and then, for most other workers in interstate commerce, by the National Labor Relations Act of 1935.

Between the adoption of these two far-reaching laws, the Federal Anti-Injunction Act of 1932 expressed public policy in favor of the right to organize and bargain collectively, and limited the issuance of injunctions by federal courts that would interfere with these rights. It became public policy to restrain the judiciary from preventing workers from exercising full freedom of self-organization and collective bargaining.

New Jersey has not adopted a state equivalent of the National Labor Relations Act, although there were efforts to get one through the legislature. One of the most recent was the attempt backed by Governor Robert B. Meyner in 1957 when he declared that "a state labor relations act is desirable in the interests of industrial justice and labor management peace." *

Although the State does not have a labor relations law it has sanctioned the right to organize and bargain collectively for workers in private industry. Public employers are also protected in the right of self-organization but this does not include bargaining collectively and striking to enforce demands. Article I of the Constitution of 1947 reads:

Persons in private employment shall have the right to organize and bargain collectively. Persons in public employment shall have the right to organize, present to and make known to the State, or any of its political subdivisions or agencies, their grievances and proposals through representatives of their own choosing.

Thus, workers in New Jersey are protected by federal law, if the employer falls within the definition of inter-

* New York Times, Jan. 9, 1957.

state commerce, or by the State Constitution if the employer is in intra-state commerce or in an industry exempt from federal regulation. A leading example of an exempted industry is hospital service. Indeed, over half of the nation's hospitals are exempt from federal law because they are owned by voluntary organizations, and hospital service, measured by employment, is the fifth largest industry in the nation.

Since no state labor relations board has been established to effectuate the rights of workers to organize guaranteed by the State Constitution, the State judiciary has asserted its jurisdiction and has declared its intent to implement the constitutional guarantee. In point of fact, though not at law, the New Jersey State Board of Mediation also contributes to carrying out these rights when the parties disputing a union's representative status voluntarily use the Board's machinery to conduct a representation election. Usually, the Board of Mediation conducts three to four elections a year. It has not sought to fill the vacuum created by the absence of a state labor relations board.

The state courts have acted in a number of instances to assert jurisdiction and implement the constitutional guarantee of self-organization.

In 1959, in a case involving an independent union of Dairy Workers and the Teamsters * the Supreme Court of New Jersey asserted jurisdiction declined by the National Labor Relations Board. It thereby prevented a "no-man's" land between federal and state jurisdictions in which the outcome would be left to an economic trial of strength.

To protect the right of freedom of choice in union representation, the Supreme Court upheld an injunction to prohibit picketing by the Teamsters aimed at dislodging a recognized, bona-fide union holding a genuine agreement with an employer. Significantly the Court concluded that a privately-held representation election es-

* Independent Dairy Workers of Hightstown v. Milk Drivers and Dairy Employees Local No. 680 (1959), 30 New Jersey Reports, 173.

tablished the independent union's status as the bargaining agent for the employees.

Chief Justice Joseph Weintraub declared that, "If Local 680 had wished to question the election . . . the Chancery Division would have been equal to the issue. It could have ordered another election with such protective provisions as would be appropriate to assure an uncoerced result." Clearly, therefore the Courts themselves were prepared to set up bargaining units, order elections, certify the results, and thus determine the employees' bargaining representation.

In 1964, in *Johnson* v. *Christ Hospital*,* the Superior Court, Chancery Division, did apply the election remedy. For this reason and because the Court declared employees of voluntary hospitals to be private employees, and therefore subject to the constitutional protection of self-organization granted private employees, the decision is of far-reaching significance.

Now New Jersey Courts will be faced with such knotty issues, usually handled by labor relations boards, as the unit of employees appropriate for bargaining (whom to include and exclude); what percentage of employees must sign union cards before an election will be ordered; and—the most difficult of all—whether once bargaining arangements have been made, the parties are bargaining "in good faith." It is evident that a Pandora's box has now been opened, suggesting that a state labor relations law is overdue in New Jersey.

Another range of labor relations problems which the New Jersey Courts must confront in implementing the constitutional guarantee of self-organization to privately employed workers is indicated by the *Nutley Sun Printing* case ** of 1961. In that case the Chief Justice of the

* 84 N.J. Super. 541, A. 2d. (Ch Dix. 1964). The author wishes to acknowledge his debt to Miss Miriam Nussbaum, of Rutgers Law School for material about and the implications of this case. It is taken from case comment to be published in the *Rutgers Law Review*.

** *James Cooper* v. *Nutley Sun Printing Co.* (1961), *Atlantic Reporter*, 2d Series, CLXXV, 639-645.

Supreme Court held that the guarantee protected New Jersey workers not only from acts of the legislature or judiciary, but private parties as well. Thus, the Court must, in effect, determine what the National Labor Relations Act proscribes as unfair labor practices and fashion remedies to cure them. Evidently the volume of work could become a severe burden to the New Jersey judicial system.

Insofar as public employees are concerned, their rights under the New Jersey Constitution extend only to organization, not to bargaining or strikes. Thus, in a 1964 decision * the Superior Court in Camden held that while employees of the Turnpike Authority had the right to organize, they did not have the right to bargain collectively or to strike. On the other hand, while the Turnpike Authority—and other public bodies—are not obligated to bargain, such agencies have an affirmative duty to meet with the employees or their chosen representatives and consider in good faith any grievances and proposals they may put forward. In addition, the Court also held that New Jersey's Anti-Injunction Act did not apply to public employees. Hence, the Court granted a permanent injunction against one of the labor organizations, the Teamsters, because it had claimed to represent some Turnpike workers, demanded recognition and collective bargaining, and threatened a strike if its demands were not met.

The bulk of New Jersey's workers are covered by the Federal labor relations law and we turn now to a brief account of that legislation and its consequences for industrial relations in New Jersey.

The crux of the National Labor Relations Act (as amended by Taft-Hartley) is in three sections: Section 7, which protects the right to organize and bargain col-

* In re, N.J. Turnpike Authority and N.J. Highway Authority vs. Am. Fed. of State County and Municipal Employees, Local 1511 and the International Brotherhood of Teamsters, Local 723, Docket No. C-1087-63, April 29, 1964, Sup. Ct. of N.J., Chancery Div., Camden Co.

lectively; Section 8 (a) and (b) which prohibits employer and union practices interfering with the rights in Section 7; and finally, Section 9, which provides a method, the representation election (and decertification election) to determine whether workers want a union and which union if they do want one. Administration is vested in the National Labor Relations Board whose powers are remedial, not punitive. Enforcement of Board orders is left to the federal courts.

The NLRB is represented in northern New Jersey by the Twenty-second Region with a Regional Director and the Regional Counsel located in Newark. From 1935 to the establishment of the Newark office in 1957, northern New Jersey was administered by the Second Region of the NLRB, located in New York City. The southern part of the state has been within the jurisdiction of the Philadelphia Regional Office from 1935 to date.

The Second Region of the NLRB played a vital role in the organizing activities of unions in northern New Jersey during the crucial years following the validation of the Wagner Act by the Supreme Court in April, 1937, to the onset of World War II. Thus, from 1937 to 1940 inclusive, the Second Region processed over five thousand cases involving elections and charges of employer unfair labor practices. Over the same four-year period the Region conducted almost 700 representation elections in which over two hundred thousand valid votes were cast.

Destpite this vigorous activity, Wiliam Carney, President of the State CIO, accused the Regional Director, Mrs. Eleanor Herrick, of stalling on charges filed by the CIO. The charges are all the more incomprehensible in view of the continuous attacks made on the NLRB and its staff by leading figures in the American Federation of Labor for being pro-CIO and undermining the craft basis of organization! Thus, at about the time Carney was attacking the New York Regional Director of the Board, John P. Frey, President of the Metal Trades

Department of the AFL told the delegates of the New Jersey State Federation of Labor in 1938,

That the decisions of the National Labor Relations Board determining what the proper body is for collective bargaining are as threatening and as dangerous to our trade union movement as the injunctions which were issued from which we suffered before we succeeded in having Congress enact the Norris-LaGuardia Anti-Injunction Bill.*

Since its inception in 1957, the Newark, or Twenty-second Regional Office of the National Labor Relations Board, has processed a number of cases which have had national significance.

Among the representation cases which arose in the Newark office and which established a national pattern is the *Sav-on Drugs* case decided in September, 1962.** The company, with nine stores in New Jersey and New York, contended that the unit appropriate for bargaining should include all its stores, or at least all those in New Jersey. However, Retail Clerk Union, Local 1262, AFL-CIO, took the position that only the store in Edison (in which it had a following) should constitute the bargaining unit. Hitherto, the National Labor Relations Board had ruled that all divisions of a retail chain which were part of a single administrative or geographic area had to be included in a single bargaining unit. Now the Board decided to apply to retail chain stores the policy which they had applied to non-retail, multi-plant operations.

The significance of the change is to facilitate organizing in retail chain stores since unions can now select only those units in which they have a following.

In another landmark case arising in the Newark Office,

* New Jersey State Federation of Labor, *Proceedings of Convention, 1938,* 75-76.
** U.S. National Labor Relations Board, *Decisions and Orders* (Washington, 1962), CXXXVIII, p. 1032.

the National Labor Relations Board strengthened the hand of a union representing employees, by preventing another union from attempting to displace the incumbent, even though the existing labor agreement contains an illegal clause. This situation arose in the *Food Haulers* * case decided March, 1962. In this case the Teamsters had an agreement which contained a provision stating

It shall not be the duty of any employee nor shall any employee be required to cross a picket line, and refusal of any employee at any time to cross a picket line shall not constitute insubordination nor cause for discharge or disciplinary action.**

The Taft-Hartley Act forbids a secondary boycott, such as observance of this clause would impose, and until the present case, the National Labor Relations Board would not allow an agreement containing an illegal clause to bar the way of a union wishing to challenge the incumbent. Since the *Food Haulers* decision, however, the Board does bar a challenge by a rival despite an illegal clause in an agreement.

The record of NLRB representation elections in the United States, New Jersey, and the Middle Atlantic Region from 1946 to 1963 inclusive, shows a steadily declining trend of union successes (p. 216). The chart reveals that unions in New Jersey typically fared better than unions nationally or in the other Middle Atlantic States, New York, and Pennsylvania, because of good showings by unaffiliated unions in this state.

The record of union victories and losses (by affiliation) in New Jersey are seen in Chart 2 (p. 218). The chart indicates, union victories in NLRB elections generally rose and fell with the number of elections, but over the

* U.S. National Labor Relations Board, *Decisions and Orders* (Washington, 1962), CXXXVI, 394.

** U.S. National Labor Relations Board, *Decisions and Orders* (Washington, 1962), CXXXVI, 394 at 395.

span of years, 1946-1963, the number of defeats grew. Of particular significance is the increasing share of defeats of AFL, CIO, and AFL-CIO unions in New Jersey. Independent unions, especially since 1958, have done far better than affiliated unions. Since December, 1957, the Teamsters have been independent, so much of the good showing of the independent group in New Jersey can be attributed to the Teamsters.

Among the reasons for the rising trend of union losses are the increased share of elections in small units, which unions typically find hard to win, the historic reluctance of white-collar workers to join unions, the bad image unions have acquired as a result of the growing allegations and evidence of corruption, and perhaps a growing disenchantment among unorganized production workers with union representation.

THE TAFT-HARTLEY ACT AND UNION GROWTH

In 1947, the Taft-Hartley Act was passed amending the Wagner Act and creating new labor legislation. In contrast to the general agreement that the Wagner Act assisted the growth of the unions, there is considerable controversy over the effects of the Taft-Hartley Act. Trade unionists in New Jersey and the Nation are convinced that the law has stopped union growth and is responsible for the union's decline in membership. However, in our judgment, the Act and its interpretation by the National Labor Relations Board during the Eisenhower Administration had, at most, only a marginal effect on the growth of union membership.

We suggest that other factors, primarily economic ones, account for the downturn in membership and the drop in the percentage of the organized labor force and non-farm employment which the union movement in New Jersey and the country have experienced.

The first of these factors has been the long-run decline of employment in the highly unionized railway transportation and coal mining industries. The drop in railway employment (excluding executives) since World War II approaches 700,000 workers. As the industry is from 90 to 100 per cent unionized, it is clear that the total drop in union membership also approaches 700,000. In addition, since the railway unions are not even subject to Taft-Hartley, their postwar membership losses are obviously unrelated to the Act.

In coal mining, the shrinkage of employment since the War due, in part, to the great increase in the substitution of oil and gas for coal, and also to the extensive substitution of machines for men, is not far below 300,000, which is about the size of the corresponding loss of the United Mine Workers' membership for the same period. Thus, if we combine the losses of the United Mine Workers and the unions in railway transportation, the overall drop in the two industries together since 1945 comes to about one million members.

As for the effect of the Taft-Hartley Act on the UMW's membership, John L. Lewis apparently so scorned the law that he refused to sign a non-Communist oath and to file financial reports with the Secretary of Labor. Furthermore, coal mining was so highly organized that whenever the miners struck in post-World War II years, they seldom bothered to use pickets to keep off possible non-union replacements, a practice not often found in other industries.

The growth of non-union, white-collar occupations is the second reason for the decline in unionism. Within the twenty years from 1940 to 1960, "white-collar" workers (professional and technical workers, managers, clerical and sales workers) have grown so rapidly in number as to increase their share of the occupational structure of employment from one-third to more than two-fifths. In the same period, manual occupations, remained at a virtual standstill, and agricultural occupations shrank to one-third of their former share.*

* M. Rutznick and S. Swerdloff, "The Occupational Structure of U. S. Employment, 1940-1960," *Monthly Labor Review*, Nov., 1962, 1211.

For union membership, these developments had far-reaching effects. Long before the Taft-Hartley Act, both the white-collar and agricultural sectors were predominantly non-union, and although the decline of agricultural employment has not adversely affected the position of American unions, the rapid growth of white-collar employment unquestionably has. For as membership has fallen in secularly declining industries, unions have been unable to compensate for these losses with new organization among the fast growing white-collar occupations.

Next, the effect of conversion from war- to peacetime production and employment after World War II and the Korean War show up in unions with large memberships in aircraft and other types of military equipment. Two unions in New Jersey and the Nation which were typical of this development were the Auto Workers and the Machinists. Thus, the Auto Workers reached a World War II high of 1,065,100 members in 1944, then declined to an interwar low of 673,200 in 1946. The union had almost regained its previous peak membership early in the Korean War, 1951, and then had pushed to an historic record of 1,417,000 in the last year of that war, 1953. Thereafter it declined with the shift from war- to peacetime production.

Similarly, the Machinists dropped from 728,000, a record membership in 1944, to an interwar trough in 1949 of 554,200, then rose to a Korean War high of 746,800 in 1953. Thereafter, this union also declined in membership.

In shipbuilding, as previously noted, the Boilermakers and Ship Builders, AFL, and the Marine and Shipbuilding Workers, CIO, spurted ahead in membership between 1939 and 1944, but thereafter, both unions took sharp losses in membership as ship construction was curtailed. Local 16 of the CIO Shipbuilders in Kearney, for example, saw its membership swell from about 6000 in 1940 to 23,000 in 1942. With the end of the war its membership returned to peacetime levels. As the Korean War did not revive America's ship construction industry, there was no marked growth in the membership of these unions during that conflict. Since 1953 both unions have continued to lose ground.

Finally, the lack of full employment, the increasing pace of technological unemployment changes in the structure of the economy, and the migration of industry from New Jersey to other sections of the country have combined to reduce further union membership in the state. Since 1947 there has been a fairly steady movement of textile, chemical, electrical machinery, and metal fabrication employment out of the state, with much of it going south.

These economic changes have hit the former CIO affiliates particularly hard because their strength is greatest in manufacturing. Technological changes in building and in printing portend similar developments among the old-line craft unions in these industries, although their impact is as yet less noticeable.

REGULATION OF UNIONS

Mounting evidence of mis-use of responsibility by union officials led to the enactment of the Labor-Management Reporting and Disclosure Act of 1959. This was the first major step government had taken to regulate the internal affairs of unions. Its central feature is a Bill of Rights for union members. These are meant to assure, first, equality for all members in nominating candidates for union office, voting in union elections, attendance at meetings, and a voice in the union's activities; second, freedom of speech and assembly with reference to union meetings; third, balloting on changes in union dues and fees, and the levying of assessments with the rights to a notice of voting on these issues; fourth, the right to sue and testify against the union in judicial or agency proceedings after using all internal union procedures; and finally, protection against unwarranted disciplinary action by union officers.

Other sections of the law add to the member's rights

in his union. These protect him from violence in the exercise of his rights; give him free access to union policy-making, financial information, inspection of contracts, and information on the provisions of the law itself; provide for the recovery of mis-appropriated union assets; and grant the right to sue the union for illegal use of trusteeships.

In general, the Secretary of Labor has wide powers to discover violations of the new law created by the Act, except with respect to the Bill of Rights and some of the additional protection given members listed above. In these matters, the union member himself must take the initiative, thus putting a heavy burden on those who would challenge entrenched power.

Nevertheless, such actions have occurred, and indeed, the first case in the national involving violation of the elections procedures took place in New Jersey. In 1960, a pro-Hoffa group of officers of the Independent Petroleum Workers Union, representing the workers of the Esso Refinery at Bayway, had their elections voided as a result of the Act. The suit charged that too many ballots had been printed in relation to the number of voters; that the officers had access to the ballots; that the arrangement for collecting the marked ballots routed them to the union's post office box for which the president alone had the key; and that the ballots had been collected before the arrival of observers and prior to the agreed-upon time.*

Similarly, the elections of the International Brotherhood of Electrical Workers, Local 1470, at Western Electric, to choose a successor to an individual who went on to become the Deputy Commissioner of Labor of New Jersey, and other union officials, have been challenged by the U. S. Secretary of Labor. The suit contends that the elections did not provide a secret ballot to substantial numbers of members; that many had been deprived of their rights to vote for their own candidates; and that the use of proxy votes contributed to an unfair elec-

* *The Daily Journal of Elizabeth,* May 9, 1961.

tion.* It was also noted that past elections—conducted before the Landrum-Griffin Act—had been followed by similar complaints.**

Another important election case which has reached the courts for decision involves the election of Anthony Provenzano and other officers of Local 560 of the Teamsters, one of the largest and most powerful locals in the International. In an election on December 14, 1962, the local union provided one polling place for all of its approximately 13,500 members who are scattered over New York State and three counties of New Jersey. In addition, the union officials allowed improperly identified persons to vote, allowed electioneering at and near the voting place, but would not permit proper challenges of voters by authorized observers. Threats of interference and reprisal denied members freedom of choice, and finally, Provenzano and his fellow officers failed to notify all members in good standing that an election would take place. As a result of these violations, about one-half the members in good standing did not vote, and Provenzano and his slate were elected to office.

On the following day, December 15, 1962, some members in good standing filed a protest with the secretary-treasurer of the local in accordance with the union's constitutional provisions. It was then referred by the local's executive board to Teamster Joint Council No. 73, the next higher body in the Teamsters' organization. The President of the Joint Council was the same Anthony Provenzano, so it was no surprise that the Trial Board which reviewed the complaint dismissed it. Thereupon, the protesting members filed an appeal with the International Executive Board. However, James Hoffa and the Board (of which Provenzano was also a member) rendered no decision within the allowable time. Having thus exhausted all internal remedies, the complainant members then turned to the U. S. Secretary of Labor for assistance.

* *Newark News*, Dec. 15, 1962.
** See *Derling* vs. *DiUbaldi*, 59 N.J. Super. 400 (1960).

The Secretary of Labor, like the complainant members, soon discovered many obstacles in his effort to gain access to the records of Provenzano's local. It finally took a court order, itself obeyed at first only in part, before the Secretary of Labor was able to secure the records and evidence to petition a court on June 3, 1963 to set aside the union election of December 14, 1962.

After being re-elected to the presidency of Local 560 of the Teamsters, Provenzano was also re-elected to the presidency of the Teamsters Joint Council No. 73 of New Jersey in May of 1963, although he had just previously been found guilty of extorting over $17,000 from a trucking firm. At the time of election, he was out on bail.*

The Landrum-Griffin Act also protects local unions from unwarranted interference by the parent national or international union. Before the Act the parent union could intervene in the affairs of a local by imposing a trusteeship. Local members and officers could obtain relief outside the unions only by difficult and costly court action. Now the Act supervises and regulates trusteeship behavior.

Protection of the financial interests of the membership and the union is now afforded by the law. In a recent case a Federal Grand Jury indicted the treasurer of District 7 of the United Rubber Workers for embezzlement, destruction and concealment of records, false entry in a financial report, and misrepresentation of reports.**

The proportion of cases handled by the Area Office of the Bureau of Labor-Management, Welfare Reports since September, 1959, when the law became effective and April, 1964, approximates New Jersey's share of total membership. The Bureau handled some 620 cases compared to about 16,000 nationally or about 4 per cent of the total which is also New Jersey's share of total membership of American unions in 1960.

* *Newark Star-Ledger,* Jan. 22, 1964.
** *U.S.* v. *Eugene Bal,* U.S. District Ct., Dist. of N.J., filed April 22, 1964.

Strikes and lockouts accompany economic development and become more critical the greater the dependence of all economic units on the market for goods and services. Strikes, the most important cause of work stoppages, are typically called by unions, although as we have seen in textiles many have originated in the frustration of dissatisfied unorganized workers. The causes of strikes vary. Some are economic, that is, arise from union efforts to raise wages, shorten hours, and the like; but they can arise from attempts to form a union; or they can grow out of a dispute over the meaning of an agreement.

Whatever the cause of a strike, the loss of output, income, and profits impose costs on the community. Consequently communities have evolved techniques to eliminate or reduce these "frictional effects." New Jersey was one of the pioneers in fashioning such techniques, preceded only by Maryland,* and currently can justly claim one of the most effective mediation services in the nation.

Nineteenth-century machinery to settle disputes involved arbitration but in included collective bargaining, mediation, conciliation, and arbitration as currently defined. It therefore was all inclusive, not specialized in its function as is present-day machinery.

Two years after Maryland created a board of arbitration (1878), New Jersey adopted a statute encouraging voluntary arbitration (as currently defined) on a local basis. Perhaps the great railway strike of 1877 and the cotton textile strike of Paterson in 1878 spurred these initial efforts to find means of avoiding strikes. The New Jersey Act of 1880 did not, however, provide either for the administration or enforcement of arbitration. The law was dormant and remained ineffective even after amended in 1886.

* William M. Weinberg, "An Administrative History of the New Jersey State Board of Mediation" (Unpublished doctoral dissertation, University of Pennsylvania, 1964), 7.

In Paterson the silk industry proposed and the Knights of Labor accepted, in 1887, an arbitration board to process grievances with a ruling as the terminal step. However, for reasons not altogether clear, the board became defunct in 1888.

In 1892 a fresh attempt was made to provide mediation services through a six-member tripartite State Board of Arbitration. One member of the Board was a union man, Joseph P. McDonnell, of the New Jersey Federation of Trades and Labor Unions, AFL. At the Board's first meeting in 1892, McDonnell was chosen president.

Initially the Board had success in settling strikes, notably on the Lehigh Valley Railroad. Because it was so successful, the State Board of Arbitration became a political issue. As a result, its activities were curtailed when travel allowances were limited in 1895. Thereafter the work of the Board decreased, going out of operation altogether in 1901.

The present State Board of Mediation owes its existence to the upsurge of New Deal laws dealing with specific areas of the labor market and labor relations; the Wagner Act, the Wage and Hour Act, the Social Security Act, and the wartime machinery set up to avoid strikes and lockouts.

Prior to the establishment of the State Mediation Board in 1941, the City of Newark experimented with a mediation agency, the Newark Labor Relations Board. It handled representation issues as well as collective bargaining disputes, unlike the NLRB, to which it probably owed its name. In function, the Newark Labor Relations Board was doing at the municipal level the type of work done nationally by the Federal Mediation and Conciliation Service.

The Newark Labor Relations Board was patterned after similar boards in Toledo and Philadelphia. It was a tri-partite board, three members from labor, three from management, and four public members. The Chairman, Professor William L. Nunn of the University of Newark, later became the first director of the State Mediation Board. All board members were unpaid, while cases were handled by a paid director and staff. It had no powers of compulsion and needed the assent of both parties to a dispute to take jurisdiction of a case.

A complete record of the Board's activities from the day it began operations in April, 1937, to its termination in 1941 is not available, but there are data for the period October, 1937, to July 1, 1939.* These show that over 60 per cent of the Newark Board's cases involved the issue of union recognition, with almost three-fourths of the cases involving unskilled workers in non-manufacturing establishments—restaurants, cleaning and dyeing, retail trade, and local transportation.

By union affiliation, the AFL accounted for 47 per cent, the CIO for 45 per cent, and independent unions and unorganized workers accounted for the rest. Overall, the Board claimed it settled over 90 per cent of the cases it handled.

The Board's principal sponsor, Mayor Meyer C. Ellenstein, was defeated in the mayoralty election of 1941 by Vincent Murphy, then Secretary-Treasurer of the State Federation of Labor. Murphy ran and was elected on a labor party ticket, Ellenstein losing as a Democrat.

One of the new mayor's first actions was to terminate the Newark Labor Relations Board, much to the dismay of many labor people, especially within the CIO. The mayor stated that the newly created State Mediation Board would take over the activities of the Newark Board. While in the short run this move may have hampered the organization of unskilled workers, in the long run the State Board's activities would overlap and the need for the Newark Board would fade. Actually, the principal reason generally believed responsible for Mayor Murphy's hasty termination of the Newark Board was his political animus for Mayor Ellenstein.

* Philip C. Newman, *Labor Legislation in New Jersey* (Washington, D.C., 1934), Table VII, 57. Newman states in a footnote to this table that he was unable to acquire data after 1939 although he visited the offices of the Board.

The experience of the Newark agency and its personnel were drawn upon heavily in setting up the New Jersey State Mediation Board. Like its predecessor, the Mediation Board was tri-partite, used a professional staff covered by Civil Service, and premised its work on acceptance of collective bargaining. The Board consists of seven members, three of whom are public, and the other four of whom are usually divided between labor and management.

Generally, the New Jersey State Board of Mediation is invited into a dispute by one or both parties, although it has the power to intervene in a dispute and offer mediation or arbitration. When a case arises, the Secretary of the Board assigns it on the basis of its location, the past experience of the mediator with the parties, and his availability.

Once a mediator establishes contacts with the parties, there is no precise formal procedure for keeping in contact. Very often he awaits a notice from one or both disputants to learn if his services are needed. He can, of course, actively seek contact on his own without awaiting notification. As a rule, however, the parties will tell the mediator if they anticipate problems, often giving him specific information. For example, management may inform the State Mediator that, "On Thursday morning the company will present the union with a major pension concession. If the union counters by dropping all its economic proposals, there will be no difficulty." Likewise, the union representative may tell the Mediator that, "The union will tell the company tomorrow that it will go below the industry pattern, but it will not settle for less than five cents. If the company does not come back with at least a token settlement we will be ready for mediation." *

The historical trend of industrial disputes under which the Mediation Board operates is favorable by com-

* William Weinberg, "An Administrative History of the New Jersey State Board of Mediation" (Unpublished doctoral dissertation, University of Pennsylvania, 1964), 74.

parison with national experience. While the State has had a slightly higher proportion of workers involved in disputes than its share of non-farm wage and salary employment in the years since the end of World War II, in terms of man-days lost New Jersey usually is below the national average. Measured against available work-time, time lost because of strikes shows that New Jersey compared to the United States is at a virtual stand-off.

Currently, the most difficult problem of the New Jersey State Mediation Board is its jurisdictional dispute with the Federal Mediation Board and Conciliation Service. While on its face a contest over which agency shall render services to parties in a dispute, at its root is a conflict of philosophy. Essentially the difference is one of assertiveness in a dispute: the State Mediation Board prefers to depend on the private parties resolving a dispute (a waiting attitude) while the Federal agency intercedes "more freely in disputes because of their concept of enforcement of a public role." *

Although New Jersey's policy toward disputes empha-sizes *assistance* to disputants to aid settlement, in 1946 the State saw need to prohibit work stoppages and lock-outs in public utilities. It was part of a national reaction to postwar strikes that interrupted public services and which culminated in the emergency disputes sections of the Taft-Hartley Act of 1947. The New Jersey Public Utilities Labor Disputes Act of 1946 forbade strikes in bus and railway transportation, telephone and telegraph, tunnel pipeline and water service, electric and gas power. Compulsory arbitration was to be substituted for the strike.

The most dramatic use of the law (frequently amended) was in the telephone strike of 1947. Whether the law was instrumental in resolving the dispute is dubious. Between 1946 and 1951 the law was invoked a dozen times, only once during a strike. Most observers and

* William M. Weinberg, "An Administrative History of the New Jersey State Board of Mediation" (Unpublished doctoral disserta-tion, University of Pennsylvania, 1964), 86.

commentators on the law are opposed to it, and on occasion governors have not invoked it, claiming it would be held unconstitutional. However, their hypothesis could only be tested if the law were enforced. Otherwise, it should be repealed.

STATE ANTI-INJUNCTION ACT

Court injunctions in labor disputes had been a major legal obstacle to unions in New Jersey ever since their effectiveness in halting strikes, picketing, and union organization was demonstrated in the famous Pullman case in 1894-1895. Resolutions demanding regulation of the issuance of injunctions by New Jersey's Courts of Chancery were to be found repeatedly in the proceedings of the conventions of the State AFL from the turn of the century.

Not until the New Idea men—the progressives in the Republican Party—along with some progressive Democrats took steps in the New Jersey Legislature in 1909 was any serious consideration given proposals to restrict the use of injunctions in labor disputes. In that year, James G. Blauvelt, an insurgent Republican leader from Passaic and legal counselor to organized labor, recommended that a section be added to a proposed constitutional amendment to reorganize the judiciary which would restrict the injunctive powers of New Jersey's courts.

Cornelius Ford, President of the State Federation, declared that "this amendment was of more vital importance to the welfare of organized workers than anything that has been attempted in the history of New Jersey." [*]

Samuel Gompers gave his support to the proposed amendment, urging all unions in New Jersey to put pressure on the Republican majority in the legislature to act. However, the Republican majority could not be fully persuaded and voted only to grant a minor con-

[*] Ransom E. Noble, Jr., *New Jersey Progressivism before Wilson* (Princeton, 1946), 128.

cession, the right of appeal where the court proceedings were punitive in nature and contempt of the order was committed outside the presence of the court.

Seventeen years later, in 1926, the legislature passed a law patterned on Section 20 of the Clayton Act (1914) prohibiting the issuance of injunctions against peaceful picketing. However, the Court of Chancery ignored the law, and if anything, increased the flow of injunctions.

In 1934, two years after the passage of the Federal Anti-Injunction Act, the State Federation submitted a petition with 1000 signatures to the Chancery asking it to adopt its own rules to limit the issuance of injunctions in labor disputes. For two years Chancellor Luther Campbell sat on the proposals, and then denied them on the grounds that the proposed rules would make labor a privileged class.

Meanwhile, the Chancery freely dispensed injunctions as the following example shows:

At a strike of the Caldes Restaurant in 1937, the men walked out at 11:50 A.M. and at 11:57 they were served with an injunction against the strike. The restraints ran from A to Q. Apparently the court [of Chancery] had examined affidavits and drawn up the long injunction in seven minutes.*

In March, 1940, the Executive Board of the State Federation of Labor adopted a resolution calling for the impeachment of Vice-Chancellor Maja Leon Berry, considered the most anti-labor jurist. However, the resolution went no further than to express organized labor's attitude.

The following year, however, New Jersey adopted a "little" Norris-LaGuardia Act restricting the issuance of injunctions by Chancery Courts in labor disputes. Only under special circumstances may a temporary injunction be issued. Ordinarily, Chancery may not grant injunctions to prevent a work stoppage, joining or withdrawing from an association, paying strike benefits, rendering

* Dayton D. McKean, *The Boss* (New York, 1940), 189.

lawful assistance to strikers even if on trial, and peaceful picketing, that is picketing devoid of fraud and violence. For Chancery to grant a temporary injunction, both parties must be notified in advance and then a hearing conducted. The injunction itself may last only five days and is not renewable.

In general, therefore, the New Jersey Anti-Injunction Law parallels the federal statute in form. However, its interpretation by the states' courts has not apparently followed the trend of Federal Courts' interpretation of the Norris-LaGuardia Act. Where the federal courts have carefully limited the issuance of injunction in labor disputes, the State's courts have, it appears, been far less reluctant to grant them.

The reasons which account for this stem first from courts' interpretations of the term, "labor dispute," and second, qualifications the courts have put on those acts which the law would otherwise seem to exclude from their control. As a rule, the courts have taken the position that the law merely prescribes a procedure which would prevent past judicial abuses but does not limit the Chancery's power to restrain.

Thus, if the courts find a disagreement not within their definition of a labor dispute, then, of course, they are not bound by the restraints on issuing injunctions. The Courts of Chancery have, it is alleged, also introduced qualifications of those actions for which the law prohibits the issuance of injunctions.* Nevertheless, most New Jersey employment is covered by the federal anti-injunction law and therefore federal courts, and since these have tended to be restrictive in issuing labor injunctions, the overall position of unions in the State is probably better than an analysis of state court actions alone would suggest.

* Martin L. Greenberg, "Injunctions in Labor Disputes in New Jersey," *Rutgers Law Review*, XI, No. 2, 444-464.

New Jersey's protective labor legislation was enacted in fits and starts, with much of it dating from the era of New Deal when social and labor legislation grew apace. In this, it followed a national trend, although at times New Jersey both led and lagged. Since the legislation affecting workers is so comprehensive and dates well back into the nineteenth century, only a sketch of its outlines can be set forth here.*

Among the landmarks of modern labor law in New Jersey was the Ten-Hour Law of 1851. Although permitting exceptions, the goal of a ten-hour working day was set. It also began the process of eliminating child labor even though only in certain industries: cotton, wool, silk, paper, glass, and flax manufacturing. Lacking an enforcement procedure, the Act was largely ignored, but beginning in 1883, factory inspection was added and the ban on child labor (boys under twelve, girls under fourteen) was extended. Meanwhile the Compulsory Education Act of 1885 required juveniles to complete minimum periods of education prior to employment. The chief factory inspector and his three deputy inspectors were charged with enforcing both laws, the second with the assistance of local authorities.

A Bureau of Factory and Workshop Inspection was established by act of the legislature in 1885, to broaden the scope of enforcement. In 1903, the enforcement procedure was strengthened by new legislation enabling the governor to remove the chief factory inspector for incompetence. Acting under this law, the incumbent was suspended and eventually succeeded by Colonel Lewis T. Bryant of Atlantic City in 1904. In that year he was appointed the first Commissioner of Labor in the New Department of Labor, following the abolition of the Bureau of Factory and Workshop Inspection. He held

* The writer is indebted to Mr. James A. T. Gribbin, Deputy Director, Division of Labor, Chief Bureau of Statistics and Records for materials from which most of this section is summarized.

the post (despite Democratic efforts to depose him during Wilson's administration) until his death in 1923. Support for Bryant came from the State Federation, as it did again in 1923 when Governor George S. Silzer also considered not re-appointing him.

Child labor was further circumscribed in 1903; it was prohibited to employ any person under fourteen in any workshop, factory, or mine. As we have seen New Jersey's ban enabled nearby Pennsylvania, which did not prohibit child labor in the same degree, to undercut employment standards in the state's silk industry.

Employer's liability for employees' injury or death in certain cases was initiated in New Jersey in 1909, largely as a result of agitation by the Bureau of Labor Statistics.* The State Federation and its affiliates also lent their support to that of the professionals to gain this enlightened labor legislation. Indeed, it is the professional, the successor to the middle-class reformer, to whom one must look for the primary mover in the burgeoning of social and labor legislation in the twentieth century. More than any other man, James T. Morgan, one-time chief of the Bureau of Labor Statistics, is regarded as responsible for the Workmen's Compensation Act of 1911. It is also ironic that with regard to state labor legislation, much was enacted by Republican legislatures and governors generally opposed by organized labor. It is reminiscent of similar trends abroad: one recalls the social legislation enacted by the Conservatives in Britain and that of Bismarck in Germany. Organized labor's role has been most effective in policing and extending labor legislation, perhaps even more effective than in initiating it.**

* See the discussion in, New Jersey Department of Labor and Industry, *Annual Report,* 1953-1954, xii-xviii.

** The State Federation played such a role in the "Horsman Dolls, Inc.," 7 *N.J.R.* 541 (1951), which upheld procedures of the Unemployment Compensation Commission. Had these procedures been successfully challenged, many employers would have avoided maximum experience rating thus reducing the funds of the Commission.

Wages in establishments not subject to federal law are governed by the state Minimum Wage Law. The law was enacted in 1933, but, lacking funds for enforcement, it did not become effective until 1936. The law sets minimum scales and hours on state, county and municipal contracts, and for women and minors. Since 1936, the administering agency, the Minimum Wage Bureau, later reorganized as the Bureau of Wages and Hours, has issued minimum fair wage mandatory orders covering women and minors in apparel, cleaning, dyeing, laundries, beauty salons, restaurants, retail trade, and light manufacturing.

New Jersey was among the earliest states to establish a Bureau of Statistics and Records in 1878. Massachusetts was the first state to establish such a Bureau in 1869, to be followed at intervals of one or two years by Pennsylvania, Connecticut, Kentucky, Ohio, and then New Jersey. From the Act creating the Bureau, it is clear that one of its functions was to develop data that would be useful in framing new legislation. Additional duties were gradually given the Bureau. As a result of its research activities the Bureau may be primarily credited for the enactment of legislation on child labor, factory inspection, the protection of the health of women in industry, the abolition of the truck system, and the Workmen's Compensation Act.

Gradually the state added more duties to the Bureau, the oldest agency in the present Department of Labor and Industry, and created other agencies in the area of labor. In 1904, the Department of Labor was created, replacing the aforementioned Bureau of Factory and Workshop Inspection. The re-organization was largely the result of demands by the State Federation of Labor, the Essex Trades Council, the Consumers' League, and the Children's Protective Alliance.

At the time of its re-organization in 1916, the Department consisted of eight bureaus headed by a commissioner and an assistant commissioner of labor. The Workmen's Compensation Bureau was added to the

Department in 1918. Again in 1922, re-organization consolidated the Department into six bureaus.

The present organization of the Department of Labor and Industry was achieved in 1948. Since then it has consisted of three divisions: the Department of Labor, the Division of Workmen's Compensation, and the Division of Employment Security.

Unemployment compensation was established in New Jersey as in most other states by provisions of the Federal Social Security Act. Machinery to deal with involuntary unemployment was set up in 1936. Since its inception, the adminstration and benefits of the program have improved, usually under the persistent pressure of organized labor.

Benefits for sickness or temporary disability not compensable under workmen's compensation were provided for workers under the Temporary Disability Benefits Law in 1948. The Act provides coverage during unemployment provided the worker has wage credits for previous covered employment.

From the foregoing sketch of labor law, it is evident that New Jersey and the Nation have afforded workers a substantial degree of protection and assistance. New Jersey has not usually led the way, but usually is among the leaders in social and labor legislation.

Under the common-law doctrine of conspiracy, trade unions attempting to maintain or improve the material standards of their members were held illegal. In New Jersey this doctrine was enacted into law, although few cases ever arose under the statute. Nevertheless, it apparently discouraged labor organization, and the State Labor Congress and its successor, the Federation of Organized Trades and Labor Unions succeeded in having the law repealed in 1883.

The right to join a union and to bargain collectively was legally protected by the National Labor Relations Act of 1935 and the New Jersey Constitution of 1947. Because New Jersey lacks a state labor relations board to effectuate the legal sanction to organize and bargain, the state courts have asserted jurisdiction and provided means for carrying out the law.

National Labor Relations Board elections results show that unions in New Jersey and the nation are winning a smaller share of elections each year. The Taft-Hartley Act, usually attacked by union leaders as the primary cause for the ebb in union membership, is considered by the author to be a minor factor in the decline. Economic variables appear to be the responsible factors.

A new turn in government regulation of labor relations are the provisions of the Landrum-Griffin Act of 1959. These protect individual members in relation to their union. A number of important cases involving these rights have arisen in New Jersey including the first case in the country involving the election of union officers.

New Jersey has an anti-injunction law modeled after the Federal Anti-Injunction Act, but its interpretation by the state judiciary is said to inject the courts in labor disputes far more than was anticipated.

The State has provided machinery to settle disputes since the inception of the State Board of Mediation in 1941. In addition, New Jersey has a comprehensive set of laws on workmen's compensation, unemployment compensation, payments for temporary disability, regulation of child and female labor, maximum hours and minimum wages, and the like, although it ordinarily does not lead in these fields.

VII

CIVIL RIGHTS, CIVIL LIBERTIES, AND POLITICS

U NION AND EMPLOYER violations of the civil rights of Negroes in employment have a long history in New Jersey.* Moreover, it has divided the State AFL-CIO as has no other issue. In fact, a dispute over civil rights proved to be the proverbial straw which split the State AFL-CIO. Because of discriminatory employment practices, few Negroes have ever held skilled jobs in the building, metal, and printing trades which are organized by unions of the AFL, or comparable positions in manufacturing industries organized by CIO unions.

That the issue of discrimination in employment is of long standing and of significance to a democratic society is underlined by an official report of the New Jersey Bureau of Labor and Industries in 1903:

So important is this subject [employment of negroes] that a general conviction is growing everywhere in the nation, that a careful study of conditions and needs of the negro population, a study absolutely removed from race prejudice and partisan bias, is necessary to the highest interests of both negroes and whites.**

* By civil rights we mean the freedom of the individual to engage in economic and social activities and to use his political rights guaranteed by state and federal constitutions without regard to race, color, or creed.
** W. C. Garrison, "The Negro in Manufacturing and Mechanical Industries," *Twenty-Sixth Annual Report of the Bureau of Labor and Industries of New Jersey, 1903* (Somerville, 1904), 163.

The state survey found that typically both employers and unions regarded the Negro as incapable of doing skilled work. However, historical records showed that Negroes were used in a large number of skilled trades during the era of slavery. The New Jersey Bureau reported that,

Cooley's "Slavery in New Jersey" is authority for the statement that in this state, negroes were employed as miners, iron workers, saw mill hands, house and ship carpenters, wheelwrights, coopers, tanners, shoemakers, millers, and bakers, and at other employments requiring skill and judgment before the Revolutionary War, and other colonial records show that in Pennsylvania as early as 1708, there were enough slave mechanics to make their competition severely felt by the freeman.

Furthermore, the Bureau observed, "That the Negro has the capacity to become an artistan is not a new proposition, but a fact well known all over the South where many hundreds of the race are now employed at skilled industries." *

The Bureau's survey also reported on the Negro membership in trade unions in New Jersey in 1903. At that time it found a total of 54 Negroes in a union movement which we have estimated to number over 17,000 in the New Jersey State Federation of Labor alone. Total membership in New Jersey unions in 1903, therefore, was even larger. The unions which reported Negro members are listed in the following tabulation:

Barbers	18	Leather Workers	2
Carpenters	7	Painters	2
Steam engineers	7	Printers	1
Boatmen	6	Hatters	1
Rubber Workers	5	Shoemakers	1
Musicians	3	Bottlers and Drivers	1
	Total	54	

* W. C. Garrison, "The Negro in Manufacturing and Mechanical Industries," *Twenty-Sixth Annual Report of the Bureau of Labor and Industries of New Jersey, 1903* (Somerville, 1904), 175-176, 169.

Turning to employers in manufacturing, the survey turned up few Negroes on the payroll, and an even smaller share holding any skilled jobs. The survey included the principal industries of the State. It covered 128,400 workers, or over one-half of total manufacturing employment in New Jersey in 1903.

Of 398 usable returns, 83 establishments reported using Negro labor while 292 employed none; the report failed to indicate any practice for the balance. The establishments which had Negroes on the payroll employed a total of 38,400 workers, but only 963 Negroes. Classified by skill, 729 of the 963 Negroes held jobs as common laborers, stablemen, and drivers and were employed in smaller-sized establishments, notably brick and terracotta manufacturing.

Nearly sixty years later, a nation-wide survey made by the President's Committee on Equal Employment Opportunity among 65 manufacturing firms indicated little improvement over New Jersey's practices. The 65 firms reported that of their 2.5 million employees 12,000 or 2.6 per cent of the total were Negroes.* (The percentage in New Jersey manufacturing in 1903 was just under 1 per cent). The proportion of Negroes in the labor market in 1960 was just over 10 per cent; in 1900, the proportion was probably smaller since the ratio of Negroes to the urban population was smaller at that time.**

The national survey covered leading companies in automobile, craft, and electrical manufacturing including those with collective bargaining agreements with former CIO affiliates, Reuther's Automobile Workers, Carey's Electrical Workers, and Beirne's Communications Workers.

Based on these results, the Building Trades Depart-

* Statement of C. J. Haggerty, National President of the Building and Construction Trades Department, Associated Press Wire, July 31 1963.

** Marion Hayes "A Century of Change: Negroes in the American Economy, 1860-1960," *Monthly Labor Review*, Dec. 1962, 1360, 1364.

ment of the AFL-CIO and its state and local counterparts in New Jersey have accused the former CIO unions of hypocrisy on civil rights. The CIO unions and their leaders had been openly critical of the building trades' restrictive practices, but when these results were compared to the proportion of Negroes found in all building occupations, the figures suggested that the building trades record was far better than that of the former CIO unions. Thus, a United States Department of Labor survey of the construction industry of June, 1963, showed that Negroes made up 5.3 per cent of the skilled employment—journeymen and apprentices—and 17 per cent of total construction employment.*

There is little doubt from the figures that the CIO leadership has not been able to effectuate the civil rights practices it preaches. There are many occupations in CIO-represented bargaining units in which the unions could support apprenticeship programs to train Negroes. However the Building Trades' criticism failed to note that the hiring process in manufacturing is in the hands of the employers, while in construction (despite the legal ban on the closed shop) it is administered almost exclusively by the unions. And the building unions have usually been quite willing to let Negroes fill many of the numerous unskilled common-labor jobs. Actually, the proper civil rights record to be compared is the employers' in manufacturing and the unions' in construction, and the results show that the building-trades unions come out slightly better.

Clearly, therefore, the building trades union are deeply involved in the civil rights issue. The building trades are the center for civil rights concern because construction is obtrusive and open to public view, public monies account for a substantial part of the work, and since public funds are involved, public authorities are subject to constitutional and political pressures for im-

* Statement of C. J. Haggerty, Associated Press Wire, July 31, 1963.

provement. Moreover, a substantial volume of employment is involved (in contrast to the printing trades which are also restrictive and discriminatory), and the long-standing apprenticeship practices favor relatives and friends of union members.

The building trades—civil rights controversy over equal job opportunities for Negroes centers in the long-standing practice of craft unions in building (and other trades) to limit the number of practitioners. The practice is based on economic reasoning and is the same as that practiced by enterprise monopolies: a reduction in supply relative to demand will raise the wage (price) of the labor (product) concerned.

Clearly, the building trades unions will not abandon a time-tested economic theorem in favor of an open-door hiring practice as demanded by the civil rights adherents. In fact, just the opposite policy can be expected from the unions: increased mechanization and use of finished materials in building which are reducing labor input requirements will intensify the unions' restrictive practices. Thus, technology is working against the opening of jobs to Negroes and other minorities in building trades. Likewise, any slackening in building activity will also work against the admission of Negroes.

Ethnically, the restrictive policy worked against the latest immigrants excepting the Negroes, who, of course, were among the earliest, but who have always been relegated to the periphery of American society. As the last waves of immigration have long since stopped, and now that the Negro's aspirations for equality must be met, the Negro and the exclusionary policies of the craft unions confront each other.

The resolution of the conflict would be difficult and very slow even if the best of climates prevailed. Even if unions tore up their waiting and apprenticeship lists only a few Negroes at most would gain access to building trades' labor markets because the problem is not only one for minorities, since "the majority of journeymen in the state cannot get union membership." * in these trades.

The door to employment in the building trades is the apprenticeship program, and the key is held by the unions. The unions may also admit qualified journeymen directly to the trade, but this occurs rarely. Moreover, on the few occasions it has been done, Negro craftsmen have failed to qualify. Recent examples are the three Puerto Ricans and the Negro who were permitted by Local 2 of the Plumbers Union in the Bronx to take the journeymen's test. They failed the test, observed by impartial observers, and were therefore not admitted as journeymen.

By means of the apprenticeship program, unions regulate the intake of new craftsmen. For the most part, joint committees consisting of employer and union representatives screen applicants for training. However, the actual results of the committees' selections over the years indicates that the unions usually nominate and chose those who enter the program. In some areas and trades, the union itself conducts the apprenticeship program, so that overall, it is fair to state that apprenticeship training is operated as the unions see fit.

Typically, the applicant is sponsored by a union member and very often is a relative of a member. Thus, a local of the International Brotherhood of Electrical Workers admitted that about 50 per cent of the apprentices initiated into membership are sons of members.** Other family ties personally accounted for an additional proportion so that few without a relative or other sponsor could hope to enter the union. This condition, of course, discourages others from even applying for apprentice training. In 1960 it was claimed that of 4000 trainees in the State only 14 were non-white, and although this

* Employment Commission of the Bi-Partisan Conference on Equal Opportunity, as quoted in the *Newark Star-Ledger,* November 17, 1963.

** *Report of the New Jersey Advisory Committee to the U. S. Commission on Civil Rights,* 1963.

figure is probably in error, the general conclusion is unchanged since few Negroes apply.

Both the Federal Bureau of Apprenticeship Training, which certifies the programs of the Joint Committees, and the State Department of Education, Vocational Division, which approves the establishment where the training is given and provides related instruction in local vocational schools have rules or operate under laws prohibiting discrimination in the apprenticeship training program. However, like the law prohibiting discrimination in projects using public funds, little improvement has been accomplished.

Moreover, the pace can be expected to continue at a slow rate as indicated by the recent testimony of leading building trades union officials: "Certainly we don't practice discrimination. We presently have one Negro member. . . . Our membership at the present time [1962-1963] is, I believe, 759." *

In another case reported to the Committee a union kept three Negroes on a temporary basis indefinitely in order to deny them membership.

As previously stated, the issue of civil rights led to a final showdown between the building trades and former CIO unions in New Jersey. The battle came to a head in 1963 as a result of a civil rights demonstration at the construction site of the new Barringer High School in Newark. To restrain interference with construction, the building trades unions began legal procedures for an injunction. While the case never went far enough to result in the issuance of an order, CIO leaders criticized the move as a use of a traditional anti-labor device to enforce discrimination. They threatened, too, to join the picketing. And, finally, 17 CIO leaders addressed a letter to Governor Richard J. Hughes urging a halt to construction where public funds are used and discrimination is practiced.**

* *Report of the New Jersey Advisory Committee to the U. S. Commission on Civil Rights,* 1963, 31.
** *Newark News,* Aug. 13, 1963.

The building trades' response was swift and furious. It described the statement of the CIO leaders as indicative of their "abysmal ignorance of the facts or a complete disregard of the truth of the matter." As for the injunction, the building trades described the CIO implication as "an insidious and unwarranted attack." * Furthermore, a leading AFL spokesman declared, "The result of these irresponsible actions and statements . . . may be the cause of creating dissatisfaction and disharmony among our affiliates to the extent that it could conceivably be the initial cause of breaking up our great N.J. State AFL-CIO."

In retaliation for this move and because of the persistent antagonisms between the leaders of the AFL and CIO, the two jobs held by CIO leaders in the AFL-CIO were abolished by the numerically superior AFL at the 1964 Convention. Thus, the civil rights issue proved too much for the merger of 1961.

Insofar as the law is concerned, discrimination in employment was not banned by statute in New Jersey until 1945. Long before, in 1884, the State adopted a law prohibiting discrimination in inns, public conveyances, and places of amusement. In 1949, jurisdiction over the civil rights laws of New Jersey was vested in a Commission on Civil Rights.

CIVIL LIBERTIES

If unions have violated the civil rights of Negroes in employment, they and the workers they sought to represent were long deprived of their civil liberties.** While

* Letter of Louis Vehling, President of the Building Trades and Construction Trades Council, to Vincent J. Murphy, President of the State AFL-CIO, Aug. 13, 1963.

** By civil liberties we mean the individuals' rights of freedom of speech, assembly, religion, to acquire and dispose of property, etc., which do not conflict with superior social rights or the equal rights of others. These rights are guaranteed by the federal and state constitutions and protect the individual from arbitrary actions by all branches of government.

the struggle of unions and unionists to gain what the Constitution of the United States and the Constitution of New Jersey freely granted cannot be recounted here, we shall briefly take note of the most notable battle over freedom of speech involving unions in New Jersey, the case of Mayor Frank Hague and Jersey City versus the CIO.

By use of local ordinances, deportations, and harassment, the Hague Administration sought to prevent the CIO from organizing in Jersey City. As a result, Hague and his cohorts violated the rights of free speech, due process, and equal protection of the laws of the Committee for Industrial Organization, various CIO organizations, the American Civil Liberties Union, and certain individuals. In the court case which followed, the District Court Judge, William Clark, wrote a memorable treatise on these liberties perhaps meant as a course in the meaning of human liberties for the benefit of Mayor Hague *et al.* The Supreme Court upheld the permanent injunction granted by Justice Clark restraining Hague and Jersey City from continuing their violations of civil liberties. To mark its victory over Hague, the State CIO held its Second Convention in Jersey City in 1939. No incidents of note occurred.

The numerous strikes in textiles were also accompanied by widespread violations of civil liberties. Characteristic were those committed during the Great Silk Strike of 1913. Summing up these violations, the United States Commission on Industrial Relations declared:

In Paterson, N. J., which was investigated with unusual thoroughness, and which, because of its size and location in the most densely populated section, might be considered likely to be free from such abuses, it was found that during the strike of silk workers, 2,238 arrests, charging unlawful assembly or disorderly conduct, were made, and that in all there were 300 convictions in the lower courts. Men arrested for unlawful assembly were held in bail of $500 to $5,000. The right of trial by jury was generally denied. Men were arrested for ridiculous reasons, as, for example, for standing on the opposite side of the street and beckoning to men in the mills to come out. This was the allegation on which the charge of unlawful assembly was placed against four men, and for which they were sent to jail in default of $500 bail, and, although never indicated, the charges still stand against them as a bar to their rights as citizens and voters. Men were fined arbitrarily, as in the case of one who was fined $10 for permitting strikers to sit on a bench in front of his house. Not more than $25 worth of damage was done during the entire strike, involving 25,000 workers, and there was no actual violence or attempt at violence on the part of the strikers during the entire strike. Under such conditions the editor of a local paper was arrested, charged with criminal libel, for comparing the conditions in Paterson with the rule of the Cossacks; and four men who sold the paper on the streets also were arrested. The editor was tried and convicted in the lower court, but the verdict was set aside by the (New Jersey) Supreme Court, while the four men, after being held several days in default of bail, were released without trial. It is imposible to summarize the activities of the police and authorities during the strike better than by referring to the testimony of two of the leading citizens of Paterson, who said that they had resolved to get rid of the "agitators" and were ready to go beyond the law to accomplish their purpose.

New Jersey has had a long, and often unsatisfactory record of disregard of civil liberties involving trade union organization. Police courts have probably been among the worst violators of the civil rights of unionists, but only fragmentary accounts of their impact are available.

POLITICAL ACTIVITY

Organized labor seldom formed labor parties or sponsored a social theory antagonistic to capitalism. When unions in New Jersey did establish a political party, they did not challenge capitalism, nor for that matter, did their party endure.

Generally, the principal efforts of unions in New Jersey were directed to supporting individuals and established political parties who shared labor's goals. More recently, some unions, especially the former CIO unions, have gone beyond these limited objectives to support the welfare state.

As we have noted, the Newark unions formed short-lived political parties in the early 1830's. A more successful Workingmen's Party was organized in Trenton and functioned from 1847 to 1855, but this appears to have been more a middle-class reformist group than a labor one.

The rise of the AFL put an end to any further serious efforts to establish a labor party since its philosophy, "support your friends and punish your enemies," came to dominate organized labor's point of view. The trade unions limited political aims were graphically delineated by Adolph Strasser, president of the International Cigar Makers Union, and one of the founders of the AFL, in testimony before the United States Senate Committee on Education and Labor in 1885. In reply to a question on organized labor's ultimate goals, Strasser replied, "We have no ultimate ends. We are going on from day to day. We fight for immediate objects—objects that can be realized in a few years." * Certainly, this came to be the philosophy and method of the New Jersey State Federation of Labor. Like its parent organization, it typically endorsed candidates and issues rather than parties. For example, in 1902 the Essex Trades Council amended its constitution to promote the discussion of politics by its affiliates; and in 1908, the Union County Trades Council drew up a legislative program which candidates were expected to endorse in exchange for political support.

The political awareness and participation of organized labor in New Jersey received a substantial boost during Governor John F. Fort's administration (1908-1911). George L. Record, one of the leading progressives in the State campaigned vigorously to "arouse organized labor

*Quoted in Foster Rhea Dulles, *Labor in America* (2nd rev. ed.; New York, 1960), 150.

to the opportunities offered by the new direct primary law," by which, he told the Union County Trades Council in 1908, the workers "can absolutely control the legislature of New Jersey and the government of every leading city of the state." *

Increased union participation, Record believed, would lay the foundation of a "strong political alliance between organized labor and the New Idea." ** (The New Idea men were progressives who appealed to liberals in both major political parties.) Perhaps as a result of this encouragement, Cornelius Ford, a Democrat, and President of the State Federation of Labor, ran for and was elected to the Assembly in 1910.

However, Record's proposal led to little effective political activity. Nevertheless gains were made in legislation, notably in strengthening the child labor law in 1910. The bill was introduced by New Idea men and progressive Democrats and supported by organized labor, civic and religious groups.

The New Idea men and their allies, progressive Democrats, with the support of the State Federation of Labor also attempted to enact a modern workmens' compensation law in 1910 but failed. Nevertheless, they forced the establishment of a commission of inquiry which did lead to an effective workmen's compensation act in 1911 under Woodrow Wilson's Administration.

The State Federation supported Woodrow Wilson in his election to the governorship in 1911 and to the Presidency in 1912 and 1916. Cornelius Ford, President of the Federation, was named Public Printer of the United States in 1914 by Wilson.

An issue in Wilson's presidential campaign which had possible repercussions for organized labor in New Jersey was the trust issue: "The treatment of the Trust question in the National campaign had so emphasized

* Quoted by Ransom E. Noble, Jr., *New Jersey Progressivism before Wilson* (Princeton, 1946), 121.

** Ransom E. Noble, Jr., *New Jersey Progressivism before Wilson* (Princeton, 1946), 122.

the ends of New Jersey corporation charter laws, as to lead the Nation to expect him [Wilson] to begin his national reform work right at home." *

Organized labor, particularly those members affiliated with the American Federation of Labor, fearing that a proposed new state anti-trust law might subject them to restraint of trade violations, had an amendment offered which would prevent the proposed law from being construed as "to make any agreement or combination relating to the hours of labor . . . or to the increase of wages . . . or any agreement affecting the hours, wages, sanitary or other conditions of labor, a violation." **

Samuel Gompers traveled from Washington to arrange for the passage of the amendment. Ford, the logical sponsor, stayed in the background in order not to "embarrass Dr. Wilson's trust schemes in New Jersey with his personal interference." † Henry F. Hilfers, Secretary of the State Federation, was therefore given the duty of seeing the amendment enacted. However, the legislature took no action.

The National AFL reversed its historic policy on endorsing political parties, and supported the Progressive Party and Robert La Follette's candidacy for President in 1924.

However, the New Jersey State Federation of Labor did not follow its parent Federation. Theodore Brandle, President of the New Jersey Building Trades Council, and his political ally, Mayor Hague, supported the National Democratic Ticket and therefore opposed La Follette.‡ Learning that the garment, tobacco, hat, brewery, and machinists unions were planning to endorse La Follette at the annual convention in September, Brandle

* William E. Sackett, *Modern Battles of Trenton* (New York, 1914), II, 363.

** William E. Sackett, *Modern Battles of Trenton* (New York, 1914), II, 363.

† William E. Sackett, *Modern Battles of Trenton* (New York, 1914), II, 368.

‡ Most of the discussion on Mayor Hague which follows is based on Dayton D. McKean, *The Boss* (Boston, 1940).

had all the building trades send delegates to the convention, and by a close vote passed a resolution banning any political endorsement.

Politically, Brandle and Hague became major factors in State politics during the twenties. Hudson County, under the Hague Machine and in alliance with Brandle's building trades, was able to elect a number of Democratic governors. In fact, majorities of a hundred thousand or more votes for Hague candidates became standard in Hudson County.

So close was the association between Brandle and Hague that when Hague was forced to pay back federal income taxes of $60,000 in 1930, Brandle's personal check was used to make payment. The arrangement was described as a loan which Hague later declared—after he and Brandle had become enemies—was repaid.

Eventually, Brandle apparently came to be regarded as a rival or threat by Hague. He had powerful support in the union movement, as well as money. The break between the two reportedly began during the building of the Jersey City Medical Center in 1931. Shortly afterward, in the construction of the Pulaski Skyway, although Hague stated that he and Brandle were still friends, the breach opened wide. Contractors using non-union labor were able to hire guards to protect their employees from Brandle's men, something the Jersey City police never before tolerated, and then the police began arresting Brandle's unionists. Brandle himself was denounced by Hague as a "labor racketeer." Brandle's efforts to stop the construction of the Skyway with non-union labor ended in personal ruin for him. He spent his entire fortune, it was reported, on strike relief, on a private hospital to care for injured strikers, and on legal fees.

Hague then turned his full political power on all unions within his reach. Many were driven into financial receivership. So completely did he wreck the union movement in Jersey City that there appears not to have been a single successful strike between 1931 and 1937. At the same time an intensive advertising campaign was undertaken to attract new industry to Jersey City, the purport of which was that newcomers would be free of "labor troubles" and "labor racketeers."

When the CIO appeared in Jersey, beginning in late 1936, organizers quickly felt the full brunt of Hague's labor philosophy. Picketing was prohibited, organizers attempting to tell workers of their rights under the National Labor Relations Act were prevented from speaking or deported, distribution of leaflets was forbidden or stopped—in short, the CIO was not permitted to function in Jersey City.

The New Jersey State Federation of Labor "in its hatred for the CIO forgot about Brandle—and supported the Mayor in his campaign against the Reds." * Robert Lynch, President of the Hudson County Building Trades Council, described Mayor Hague as the "protector of the people" and praised him unblushingly.

Leading members of the business community joined in the accolades, but in the end the Supreme Court required Hague to stop his practices.

The jubilant State CIO, through William J. Carney its president, declared that "the Hague machine is cracking" and that the CIO in Hudson County would use its political power "until Hague is either in jail or political oblivion." ** Nevertheless, two months after these declarations, the UE faction of the CIO, which dominated the Hudson County CIO Council, and Hague came to a political settlement. The leaders of the CIO declared that they would not be used by anti-labor Republican political bosses to defeat Hague. However, it should be noted that the leaders of the State CIO, Abramson who succeeded Carney to the presidency, and Holderman, the Secretary of the State CIO beginning in 1940, consistently opposed Hague.

The AFL took note of the denouement of a labor-political alliance in the Hague-Brandle affair, and so adopted a more independent political course. In 1934

* Dayton D. McKean, *The Boss* (Boston, 1940), 197.
** Dayton D. McKean, *The Boss* (Boston, 1940), 199.

the Federation set up Labor's Non-Partisan Leagues in Essex and Passaic counties. Its support helped elect two candidates to the City Commission of Newark by 1937, one of whom was Vincent J. Murphy, Secretary of the Federation. In 1941, it supported and helped elect Charles Edison to the governorship.

An aborted effort to enhance further organized labor's "balance of power" role in New Jersey politics was made in 1940 with the formation of the New Jersey Labor Party. While active in the 1940 presidential election, it failed to gain the endorsement of the State Federation, although it did receive the support of State CIO. Because the AFL and other important labor groups did not back it, the Labor Party dissolved in 1941.

The political power of the union movement in New Jersey was strong enough in 1943 to bring the Democratic Party's nomination for governor to Vincent J. Murphy, Secretary-Treasurer of the AFL, Mayor and former councilman of Newark. However, Murphy lost the race. He retained the mayoralty of Newark until 1949.

His nomination for governor came about as a compromise when Hague's candidate, Senator A. Harry Moore, was blocked by a combination of forces including Governor Edison and the CIO. The CIO later charged that Hague undermined Murphy's campaign "to teach labor a lesson." * Organized labor, however, buried its differences sufficiently to form an ABC Labor Federation Committee (*A*FL, Railway *B*rotherhoods, *C*IO) consisting of five representatives from each of the three labor groups to support Murphy.

Although the State AFL and CIO did join to support Murphy's bid for the governorship in 1943, typically the two groups were at variance on political philosophy, methods, candidates, and, frequently, on issues as well.

There was some cooperation between the AFL and CIO between 1936 and 1942 in Labor's Non-Partisan League of New Jersey, a branch of the national League.

* *New Jersey CIO News,* July, 1949.

Increasingly, however, it was run and dominated by the CIO, in the person of Carl Holderman, so AFL participation gradually diminished. The national League was run by John L. Lewis.

Splits within the League developed over President Roosevelt's bid for a third term in 1940. Holderman and the majority of the League supported the President, but Lewis opposed him for personal reasons and because, as an isolationist, he was against Roosevelt's foreign policy, then actively supporting Britain. The Communists also opposed Roosevelt's foreign policy at this time for reasons explained above. They joined Lewis and also opposed the League's policies. Since the United Electrical, Radio and Machine Workers, CIO was under the control of Communist Party followers, and since the union dominated the Greater Newark Industrial Union Council, they put the Council on record defying the League's orders to support the President.

A year and a half later, by May, 1942, the Communist Party line had shifted to support the war effort (after the invasion of Russia in June, 1941), so the Communists supported a move recommended by Holderman to sever the New Jersey League from the Lewis-controlled national League. Thus, a local of fur dressers and dyers in Newark, a union which was also Communist dominated, declared: "It is clear that he [Lewis] is attempting to form a labor front of anti-war, with discredited elements within labor itself and with elements outside labor." *

Holderman and his supporters wished to sever ties with Lewis because he had created splits in the CIO (after resigning as president following the 1940 Presidential elections) and because of his anti-Roosevelt policies.

Consequently, the League renamed itself the American Labor League of New Jersey and in effect became the CIO's political arm.

The League's program included support of Governor Charles Edison, revision of the State Constitution, lend-

* *New York Times,* May 25, 1942.

lease, and in 1943, it aided the ABC association in trying to elect Murphy governor.

In February, 1944, the League reconstituted itself as the New Jersey CIO Political Action Committee, modeled after the national organization of the same name. Carl Holderman was named President, and Martin Gerber of the Auto Workers, Treasurer. The new organization voted to tax all CIO affiliates 1 cent per member, per month to finance its activities.

From its beginning, the New Jersey CIO Political Action Committee was far more dramatic and effective than its predecessors. It ran mock legislative sessions for its leaders and members, raised and spent great sums of money, employed hundreds and even thousands of paid and non-paid political campaigners. In 1950, for example, 750 of the Democratic Party's 6000 poll challengers were supplied by the CIO. Although smaller than the AFL in membership, the CIO's political activities were so effective that the organization wielded a political power disproportionate to its numbers.

The CIO often supported candidates opposed by the AFL. Thus, in the 1946 gubernatorial election, the CIO supported Lewis G. Hansen, a Democrat, over Alfred E. Driscoll, a move which an AFL Republican leader denounced as a sell-out to Hague. If it was a sell-out, then the CIO's support (albeit private) of the Republican Alfred E. Driscoll in 1949, in preference to the Democrat Elmer H. Wene, who was a real Hague candidate, is inexplicable. The difference between the two elections was that Hansen was not a Hague man while Wene was. Most of the top AFL leaders in the State, it should be noted, supported Wene.

In the Presidential election of 1948, the CIO belatedly came to the support of President Harry Truman. Although one of the first CIO state councils to do so, the CIO under Holderman had previously urged the Democrats to draft General Dwight Eisenhower, or Justice Wiliam O. Douglas, as their candidate. The State CIO opposed Henry A. Wallace with Holderman at one point calling on him to withdraw from the race lest he lose Truman too many votes. The Newark Industrial Council, under the control of United Electrical, Radio and Machine Workers, an organization then about to be expelled from the CIO for being Communist dominated, supported Wallace.

The AFL also supported Truman in 1948, but it is doubtful if either federation thought he could win. The attempt in 1948 to beat Representative Fred A. Hartley, Jr., co-sponsor of the law so disliked by all organized labor, failed, however. In 1949, the AFL formed a statewide equivalent of the CIO-PAC, Labor's League for Political Education. With the merger in 1961, the LLPE and CIO-PAC became the Committee on Political Education, COPE.

While both the State AFL and CIO endorsed Adlai Stevenson and the Democratic Party nationally in 1952, they split again over the gubernatorial election of 1953. The joint political action in 1952 was the first since the Vincent Murphy campaign of 1943. Curiously, it appears that the two groups could unite only when backing a loser. Thus, they renewed their alliance on behalf of a loser when they again supported Stevenson for the Presidency in 1956. Only in 1960, when the AFL and CIO supported John F. Kennedy did they jointly support a winner.*

Far more significant than the alliance for defeat, in the Presidential races of 1952 and 1956, was the political struggle of the CIO and AFL in the gubernatorial race of 1953.

Paul Troast, the Republican gubernatorial candidate in 1953 had the official support of the AFL leadership, and Meyner that of the CIO. While the State Federation had supported more Republicans than had the State

* It should be noted that both had endorsed other important winners of Congressional offices, notably Senator Harrison Williams, and successfully opposed others. We are also disregarding the elections of President Roosevelt and Truman in 1944, and emphasizing post-World War II elections.

CIO, nevertheless, its support of Troast was at first regarded as a surprise. However, when Senator Troast's letter to the New York State Parole Board on behalf of Joe Fay, boss of New Jersey's Operating Engineers and a power in the building trades who was a convicted extortioner, became known, the riddle was solved: "What Mr. Troast did for Fay, they [the Republican leaders] reason, he did at the request of labor leaders." *

Troast was known to be friendly to the building trades unions, but his letter requesting a parole for Fay doubtless gained him the support of the leadership of this group. Furthermore "to the numerous walking delegates who hovered over Fay's cell, a Troast victory would be a sure sign that New Jersey voters saw no impropriety in the mass visitation by labor and political bosses to Sing Sing." **

Evidently the voters did see improprieties and Robert Meyner won. The CIO's political power, arrayed behind Meyner, raised its leadership to new positions of influence in the state. Carl Holderman, as already noted, became Commissioner of Labor and Industry. The AFL's leaders, especially Marciante, because of their antagonism to Holderman, and for other reasons, always opposed Governor Meyner.

The CIO supported Meyner for re-election in 1957 and Richard Hughes in 1961. Officially, the Federation was neutral in 1961, a stand regarded as favorable to James P. Mitchell, the Republican. The AFL's publicly declared reason for neutrality was that their time was needed to consummate the forthcoming merger with the CIO! Nevertheless, many top AFL leaders and groups did support Hughes. A notable example was Samuel Di Ubaldi of the IBEW's Western Electric Local. After Hughes' victory he became a Deputy Commissioner in the Labor and Industry Department.

Through the period 1956-1961, when the State CIO and AFL functioned separately, a perennial problem was the allocation of money from the national Com-

* *Newark News,* Oct. 4, 1953.
** *Newark News,* Oct. 4, 1953.

mittee on Political Education. On occasion, the National COPE by-passed both the state organizations and its leaders. On others, the national committe allotted equal funds to each State group, a practice to which the State Federation strongly objected. Federation leaders contended the allocation should have been on a basis proportionate to numbers.

While the merger "solved" the COPE problem, the recent exiling of the two top CIO leaders again raises the question of allocating money from national headquarters. The N.J. AFL-CIO President, Vincent Murphy, has already declared that it is the only representative of the national movement in the state, and, has been so recognized by the National COPE. Presumably it alone will receive COPE funds.

PUBLIC RELATIONS AND EDUCATION

Today trade unions try to keep their membership informed and to present their views to the public through a substantial press and through public relations specialists. But the labor press remains sparse and of uneven quality.

In New Jersey an outstanding labor paper of the late nineteenth century was Joseph P. McDonnell's *Paterson Labor Standard*. McDonnell brought the paper to Paterson from Fall River, Massachusetts, in the course of an internal dispute among Socialists over the economic (trade union) versus the political approach to improving workers' material existence. McDonnell, an advocate of the economic approach, steadily moved closer to the trade unionists and in due course became one of the founders of the New Jersey Federation of Organized Trades and Labor Unions, the forerunner of the State AFL. At the 1890 Convention of the Federation, McDonnell's paper was endorsed as the organization's official paper. About 1904 the *Labor Standard* ceased publication and the AFL did not endorse another until the *Union Labor Bulletin* of Newark received official support in 1915.

Other labor papers functioning at this time were the *Hudson County Labor Review,* edited by Kenneth Forbes, one-time treasurer of the Federation; the *Union Labor Advocate,* published by George Reiss, printer and former secretary of the Union County Central Labor Union; the *Trenton Trade Union Advocate,* edited by Reuben Forker, who also held the post of secretary of the Mercer County Central Labor Union. In the twenties, Henry Hilfers, Secretary of the Federation, published the *Union Labor Messenger.* In Trenton, during the thirties, Louis P. Marciante, who was president of the Federation for so long a period, published *The Labor News.* This was succeeded by *The Trentonian* put out by the International Typographical Union as an outgrowth of a strike of the *Trenton Times.* Later, *The Trentonian* was sold to a private publisher.

In 1939, the *New Jersey Labor Herald* began publication under the direction of Lewis M. Hermann, well-known member of the ITU, Republican officeholder, and member and Secretary of the International Labor Press Association. The *Herald* was officially endorsed by the State Federation. The CIO published its own paper, *The New Jersey CIO News.* Since the merger, a new journal has not been issued by the State AFL-CIO.

The New Jersey State AFL-CIO maintains a Community Services Committee to coordinate its relations with the community but also carries on numerous activities that fall outside it as well. In addition, affiliates also maintain programs of their own. Thus, New Jersey district of the International Union of Electrical Workers aids volunteers who wish to enter the Peace Corps. Other unions have had programs dramatizing the campaign against poverty at home and abroad, and one has initiated a Mankind Day.

The AFL, the CIO, and the AFL-CIO have given their moral and financial support to the Institute of Management and Labor Relations at Rutgers University. The Institute was established under the administration of Governor Alfred E. Driscoll in 1947, with the bill offered by Assemblyman Lewis Hermann, publisher of the *Labor Herald*. Most of New Jersey unions have made use of its facilities. Organized labor supported and helped obtain a Labor Education Center at Rutgers, one of the first on any campus.

The violation of Negroes' civil rights in employment in New Jersey has a long history. While Negroes are still mainly confined to unskilled jobs, recently the civil rights issue has become a major area of contention between AFL and CIO unions in the New Jersey AFL-CIO. Because of CIO criticism of AFL building trades apprenticing practices, (and for other reasons), in June, 1964, the numerically larger AFL abolished the two leading jobs in the merged federation which were held by CIO men. As a result, the split in the State's union movement has been re-established in fact if not in name.

Violations of the civil liberties of New Jersey unions and workers have been frequent and go back a long time, too. The silk strike of 1913, although relatively unmarked by violence, was characterized by widespread violations of civil liberties.

Mayor Hague in the decade of the 1930's attacked both the AFL and the CIO. The intensity of his attacks on the CIO led to flagrant violations of civil liberties which were stopped finally by order of the Supreme Court of the United States.

Unions have always played a role in politics, and this participation was greatly increased by the encouragement of progressives in the years just preceding Woodrow Wilson's election to the governorship.

Probably the most effective labor campaigns in New Jersey have been mounted by the CIO's Political Action Committee. Generally, the CIO and AFL have been at odds on political philosophy, methods, candidates, and even issues. It is likely that the two groups will go their separate political ways, despite the nominal re-unification of April 1, 1965.

VIII

THE FUTURE OF
NEW JERSEY UNIONISM

THE UNION MOVEMENT in New Jersey, along with the national movement, can expect to lose membership in the years immediately ahead, thus extending the losses which have already been absorbed during the last decade. New Jersey unions have probably lost proportionately fewer members than have unions generally, and, therefore, the slippage in the extent of the labor market organized has likewise been less in this state than in the nation. Between 1953 and 1964, while union membership in New Jersey dropped about five per cent to the present level of approximately 700,000, the decline in the country ran to about ten per cent. Meanwhile, the proportion of the non-farm workers organized fell from over 35 to abut 33 per cent in New Jersey. In the United States, this ratio has declined much more since 1953, from approximately 33 to 26 per cent, thus reducing the national extent of organization to levels of 1942-1943.

Among the reasons for New Jersey's slower decline compared to the national shrinkage of membership and extent of organization are the absence or lesser importance in New Jersey of the declining unionized industries of coal mining and railway transportation, and, on the other hand, the stability of employment and membership in the highly unionized construction industry.

Organization of the unorganized, essential to union growth, has clearly been running into serious roadblocks in New Jersey and the Nation, as shown by the steadily falling proportion of victories won by unions in National Labor Relations Board elections. New Jersey unions, which lagged behind in the organization of industry, despite the vast gains of 1939-1953, may therefore slip back in the standing of state labor movements.*

The pessimistic forecast which we have given does not imply the disintegration of the state's union movement. It is a stable movement of considerable strength and influence. However, our forecast does seek to dispel any naïve optimism that the New Jersey union movement will continue to grow simply because it has in the past. Nor can the lapse of time be expected to dissolve all major difficulties. Indeed, left to time alone, the factors presently undercutting the state's union movement will simply reduce it even further.

Meanwhile, there are several crucial problems besetting organized labor in New Jersey which will add to the decline we have foreseen because they show no indications of being resolved. These are the impact of technology on the structure of employment, the acceptance and enrollment of the Negro in the union movement, the organization of white-collar workers, the continuing split in the New Jersey AFL-CIO, and transcending all, the crisis in union leadership.

Technology and Employment

Changes in methods of production reducing labor requirements have already contributed to the ebbing of union strength and the pace of technological change is likely to accelerate rather than diminish in the future.

* Data and conclusions on membership changes are from Leo Troy, "Trade Union Membership, 1897-1962," *Review of Economics and Statistics*, Feb., 1965; Leo Troy, Union Membership in New Jersey," *Review of New Jersey Business*, July, 1956; and files of the author.

The magnitude of job displacement caused by technological change, even by conservative forecasts, is very large. In the next decade two million jobs in the American economy will be wiped out because of improved methods of production.* Proportionately, New Jersey's share would be about seventy-five thousand, but actually it might be even higher because of the predominance of the type of employment characterized by rapid change —manufacturing—in New Jersey's economy.

Meanwhile, the kinds of jobs which will be developed are those which have not been organized in the past and show no signs of becoming unionized. In fact the job-holders demanded by the new technology are frequently either uninterested or even anti-union in outlook, as exemplified by the following example from petroleum refining:

As mechanically minded youngsters, they once would have gone into some skilled craft, that of electrician, say. They would have finished their education at high school, worn dungarees at their work and joined a craft union. Now they worked in white shirts and business suits for a salary instead of an hourly wage. They had the equivalent of two years' college training and called themselves maintenance engineers, although they had no degree. And they were hostile to unions.

"How could we strike?" one maintenance man asked. "This system must be kept going twenty-four hours around the clock." **

Technological change will alter the composition of employment in a way unfavorable to New Jersey's union movement. Well-organized industries will continue to recede in importance and industries predominately non-union will increase in importance.

Manufacturing, which for decades has been "the back-

* Ewan Clague and Leon Greenberg, "Employment," in J. Dunlop (ed.), *Automation and Technological Change* (Englewood Cliffs, 1962), 127.
** Lester Velie, *Labor USA Today* (New York, 1964), 3.

bone of this state's economy," * and has been well organized since the end of World War II, is becoming less important in New Jersey's economy. In 1947, nearly half of all non-farm jobs in New Jersey were in manufacturing industries. In 1963, manufacturing's proportion dropped to 38 per cent of the jobs.

Meanwhile, the number of factory workers in New Jersey is actually declining. While there were about 672,500 production workers in New Jersey's manufacturing industries in 1947, the number has dropped to about 565,000 in 1963. At the same time, the figures show an increase in the number of white-collar jobs in manufacturing, and, as previously indicated, these are difficult to organize.

Employment contributed by trucking, railways, gas and electric utilities, and telephones, all strongholds of unionism, also has declined somewhat since the end of World War II. Only construction, among the highly organized industries, has shown an increased share of New Jersey employment. However, it increased only one-half of one per cent between 1947 and 1963. Meanwhile, the share of blue-collar jobs in construction is falling, as is, apparently, the proportion of union jobs.

In contrast to the general shrinkage in importance of unionized industries, the industries predominately non-union in New Jersey are growing in importance. Thus, the proportion of jobs in retail and wholesale trade, finance, insurance, real estate, services, and state and local government has risen. As a group, these industries accounted for almost 39 per cent of all non-farm employment in 1947; in 1963, their share was almost one-half the total.**

County data on jobs covered by unemployment compensation in New Jersey reinforce the tides working against unionism. Between 1947 and 1956, "it appears

* Thomas J. Reynolds, "Growth and Structure of Employment," in *The Economy of New Jersey* (New Brunswick, 1958), 145.
** U.S. Bureau of Labor Statistics, *Employment and Earnings Statistics for States and Areas, 1939-1963*, Bulletin No. 1370-1.

that all but one of the older established industrial centers lost ground, relatively, to their surrounding suburban or rural areas." * Typically, rural and suburban areas are less well organized than cities.

Doubtless this trend is continuing. It is also likely that the movement away from the older centers to newer areas has been accompanied by a shift from less to more efficient plants using less labor and perhaps even changing from union to non-union conditions.

The change in occupational make-up of the work force from blue- to white-collar workers is another way of looking at the employment changes just noted. As a rule, the growth industries use more white-collar workers, and historically unions have had little success in organizing them. Similarly, if the proportion of young persons going into the labor force declines, as may well occur because of the lengthening of the educational process, this would be another factor in economic development working against unions: college graduates have shown little propensity to join unions.

The impact on the New Jersey unions is more difficult to measure than the national impact, yet it is plain enough. Thus, Richard Lynch, of Westinghouse Corporation's Bloomfield Local 410 of the International Union of Electrical Workers, cites this example:

Twelve girls who used to produce vapor lamps were replaced by a machine requiring only one maintenance man. The girls were paid $2.10 an hour; the maintenance man receives $2.88. Total annual savings in labor costs $46,426.**

Similarly, Donald Smith, Regional Director of the Packinghouse Workers said that his union has lost *half* of its membership in New Jersey because of automation.

Many other labor leaders have not seen the member-

* Thomas J. Reynolds, "Growth and Structure of Employment," in *The Economy of New Jersey* (New Brunswick, 1958), 147.

** *Sunday Star-Ledger* (Newark), April 15, 1962. The other examples which follow are also taken from this source.

ship rolls cut, but neither have they seen membership grow as output grew. In some cases the growth in employment and union membership has been far less than the rate of growth in production.

For example, Martin Gerber, Regional Director of the Auto Workers, was reported as saying that since the end of World War II auto production in New Jersey rose 60 per cent, but employment only 10 to 15 per cent, due to a gradual substitution of machines for men.

Bruno Sorchinski, representing the Newark Bakers Local, reported stable employment for his union, but also that output has risen rapidly with the introduction of new bread-making methods.

Likewise, Sam Di Ubaldi, Deputy Labor Commissioner and former president of the union at Western Electric's Kearney Plant, reported stable or slowly declining employment as workers who die or retire are not replaced. Hence employment has not kept pace with production.

In textiles, it is now possible for one man to operate thirty looms compared to four, and it will be recalled that the great silk strikes of 1912 and 1913 were provoked when the mills went from one and two looms to three and four!

Loss of industry to other areas of the country is another way which can and has cut employment and union strength in New Jersey. For example, in November, 1961, Mack Truck Company closed its 50-year-old plant in Plainfield and moved to Hagerstown, Maryland. A total of 2700 jobs were lost.

While the old Plainfield plant consisted of multi-storied, red-brick buildings sprawled over 33 acres, the new Hagerstown plant is one story and suited to automated production. In addition, the prevailing wages in Hagerstown were "far lower than in Plainfield." *

Meanwhile, the rising expectations of Negroes for equal opportunity poses severe tests for the unions, and not just those in the building trades. While some accommodation is needed in the building trades, unions in

* *New York Times,* Jan. 31, 1962.

manufacturing industries can also contribute toward raising the Negro in the occupational ladder. There are many skilled jobs in industries represented by CIO unions, and one of the prime tasks of the New Jersey State Industrial Union Council should be to encourage apprenticeship training of Negroes for jobs which its affiliates represent.

UNION LEADERSHIP

Unions in New Jersey face a crisis of leadership. The AFL wing of organized labor in New Jersey was led for more than a quarter of a century by two men, Louis P. Marciante, now deceased, and Vincent J. Murphy. Both were building trades unionists of the "old school" and provided steady, competent and shrewd leadership.

A successor to Murphy, however, does not seem to be on the scene. Hence, it is likely that his retirement will be followed by a contest for leadership of the AFL, and therefore of the AFL-CIO.

The CIO has apparently solved its factional disputes of 1960 arising out of the Paul J. Krebs–Joel Jacobson struggle for the presidency. However, the rift between Jacobson and the AFL leadership is so wide that a split between them is almost certain to persist for a long time.

The need for organizers is particularly great, but the supply is in inverse relationship to the need. Aggravating the leadership problem facing both AFL and CIO is the growing exodus of proven leaders into politics. In the nineteenth century, many labor leaders went into politics to the detriment of union organization. Perhaps that was their ultimate goal; perhaps they came to believe that political changes were vital to labor. In either case, working men lost leadership they could not afford to lose especially since leaders were so few. Is history repeating itself? Thus, Paul Krebs sought and won election as a Democrat in 1964 in the Twelfth Congressional District, joining another former CIO man, Congressman

Joseph J. Minish, Democrat, who was re-elected in the Eleventh District.

The continuing rift in the New Jersey AFL-CIO will make it very difficult for organized labor in this state to cope with the problems arising from technological change, organizing the white-collar worker and the Negro. A leader who can command general respect and unite the warring factions will be a major factor in the success of the New Jersey union movement in dealing with these problems.

President George Meany undertook steps to heal the break in New Jersey by appointing three national AFL-CIO vice-presidents, Joseph Beirne of the Communications Workers of America, Herman Kenin of the American Federation of Musicians, and Peter Schoenman of the Plumbers, to investigate and mediate the dispute.[*]

Although we have emphasized the split between the AFL and CIO in New Jersey as an adverse factor for the future, there are possibilities that the renewed competition will aid new organization rather than injure it. After all, the largest union gains in New Jersey did come in an era when the two federations were usually at odds. However, the likelihood seems to us to be that the split will injure rather than help organized labor in New Jersey.

The leadership problem of the strongest single union in New Jersey, the Teamsters, is in an even more deplorable state. The Teamsters were expelled by the AFL-CIO in 1957, nationally, because of alleged hoodlum and gangster influence. In New Jersey, Anthony Provenzano, the "boss" of the Teamsters and friend of James Hoffa, was found guilty of extortion, as previously noted, and while on bail for this conviction, won re-election to the presidency of the State Teamsters Joint Council.[**]

"Tony Pro," as he is familiarly known, has met oppo-

[*] *New York Times*, Aug. 6, 1964. As noted on p. 136, the rift has been nominally healed.
[**] *Newark Star-Ledger*, Jan. 22, 1964, and Feb. 16, 1963.

sition within the New Jersey Teamsters especially from Milton Liss, President of Local 478, but as yet the opposition looks to be a long way from power. A shotgun blast at the home of a teamster oppositionist indicates that the processes of change in the Teamsters may not be painless.* Nevertheless, in 1964, when Tony Pro was again re-elected president of Teamsters Joint Council No. 73, there had to be a run-off election and in the balloting which determined his election, 108 of 250 eligible voters abstained or were absent.**

Overall, the problem of bribery and extortion in labor relations presents such great legal difficulties that doubtless what the public sees is the iceberg phenomenon: most of it is unseen. Thus, a Hudson County Grand Jury found, in 1959, that New Jersey's laws covering bribery and extortion in labor relations, dating from 1911, can not deal with the issues.†

A corollary to the leadership crisis is the gap between intellectuals and at least part of the New Jersey union movement. Generally, ideas and intellectuals are more welcomed by the CIO than by the AFL group of unions in this state. Indeed, the present leader of the New Jersey Industrial Union Council, Joel Jacobson, is regarded as an intellectual, and it is widely believed that this contributed to the deterioration of personal relations between him and some of the AFL leadership during the short-lived merger, 1961 to 1964.

The AFL's greater wariness toward intellectuals stems from their belief that the intellectuals' ideas seldom originate from experience, and therefore are usually impractical in concept or application.

At times, intellectuals justify this attitude. For example, one labor intellectual attributed the present malaise of the American union movement to its failure to "become the champion not just of its own adherents, but of slum dwellers, migrant workers, and other Amer-

* *Newark News*, March 3, 1960.
** *New York Times*, Jan. 22, 1964.
† *Newark Star-Ledger*, Dec. 22, 1959.

icans in the lower depths," * despite the fact that the history of organized labor is strewn with wrecks of labor organizations which tried to uplift all mankind with one mighty effort. The AFL theory of bread and butter unionism, of more and more, may hold a narrow, even selfish vision of organized labor's mission in a private enterprise economy, but it has proven to be partially attainable.

In addition, the future of the union movement in New Jersey and in the country will hinge not on its ability to organize those in the "lower depths," but just the opposite spectrum of the labor market, the white collar workers. In our developing, affluent economy, the unions must hope to represent the more important "middle class" segment of the labor force, not the relatively dwindling unskilled component. History puts the question, will the AFL's past inability to unionize factory workers *en masse* be matched by the AFL-CIO's future inability to organize white collar workers?

Although there may be occasions when organized labor's skeptical attitude toward intellectuals may be justified, nevertheless we share the view that the recent growing cleavage between unions and intellectuals does contribute to the "present crisis in the labor movement, the erosion of its vitality and its membership rolls, and its prickly defensiveness toward even the friendliest critics." **

In sum, we believe that the summit of union economic and political power in New Jersey has probably been passed. While both aspects of union power remain essentially intact, it is the political power of unions which will ebb first and more rapidly: fewer members reduces union political potential.

Union economic power, however, has not suffered in proportion, because the decline of membership moved

* Herbert Harris, "Why Labor Lost the Intellectuals," *Harpers*, June, 1964, 84.
** Herbert Harris, "Why Labor Lost the Intellectuals," *Harpers*, June, 1964, 79.

along with the shrinkage of employment in unionized industries. Unions were not expelled from companies and industries as they were after World War I. Hence, in relation to employment, unions are as organized as ever.

Yet, the absolute reduction in membership must inevitably mean a chipping away of union economic power. This development is as yet in its early stages, but as the introduction of automated devices is speeded, the challenge to union strength will likewise increase.

Will the unions be able to compensate for these adverse changes by organizing the Negro and the white-collar worker? To date, significant break-throughs have not been made nor are there signs of any in the offing.

Our evaluation is not meant to suggest the eclipse of union power and influence. Far from it. Unions will continue to function as significant institutions in the economy and in the political life of the State and Nation. However, the author believes that the heights of power have already been scaled by the union movement, but that the view from its still-lofty position obscures the fact that it is now on the other side of the crest.

APPENDIX A

Constitution of the Newark Trades' Union, 1834 *
At a regular meeting of the "Trades' Union," held at
F. Moore's, in the Town of Newark, Sept. 16, 1834, the
following preamble and resolution was unanimously
adopted; Whereas the Union has been represented as
being a secret Association, therefore.

Resolved, That the Constitution and By-Laws be
published.

CONSTITUTION.

ARTICLE I.

This Association shall be called the "Trades Union
of the Town of Newark"

ARTICLE II.

The object of this Institution shall be to promote the
general welfare of Mechanics of the Town of Newark,
and to sustain their pecuniary interests.

ARTICLE III.

The business shall be transacted by regularly appointed
Delegates from each Trade, Society, or Association of
Mechanics represented.

* From Frank T. De Vyver, "The Organization of Labor in
New Jersey Before 1860" (unpublished dissertation, Princeton
University, 1934), Appendix to Chapter XI.

ARTICLE IV.

The number of Delegates appointed by each Society shall be in proportion to the number of members composing such Society as follows: each Society whose number of Members does not exceed twenty, shall be represented by two Delegates, and every Society consisting of a larger number than twenty, shall add one Delegate for each additional fifteen members, until the number amounts to fifty, after which one Delegate shall be added, for every additional twenty-five members.

ARTICLE V.

The Officers of this Union shall consist of a President, Vice-President, Recording and Corresponding Secretary, Treasurer, and a Finance Committee, all of whom, except the Finance Committee, shall be elected by ballot semi-annually.

ARTICLE VI.

Sec. 1.—The election or appointment of Delegates by the Societies herein represented, shall take place in the months of February and August, and their term of service shall commence on the stated meeting of the Union succeeding, and shall continue six months from the period of its commencement provided that nothing shall prevent Societies from withdrawing Delegates when they may deem it advisable.

Sec. 2.—Every Delegate before entering upon his duties shall subscribe to this Constitution.

ARTICLE VII.
Duties of the President.

Sec. 1.—It shall be the duty of the President to preside at all meetings of the Union—to decide all questions of order, such decision being subject to a appeal regularly made and seconded, to sign all orders given by the Union, and in case of an equal division he shall give the casting vote.

Sec. 2.—He shall call special meetings of the Union,

when requested by a majority of Delegates of three trades represented.

Duties of the Vice-President.

Sec. 1.—In the absence of the President the Vice-President shall perform all his duties.

Sec. 2.—He shall preside at all meetings of the Finance Committee, but shall not have a vote in their proceedings.

ARTICLE IX.

Sec. 1.—The duty of the Recording Secretary shall be to keep all books and papers appertaining to his office, which shall be at all times open for inspection by the Delegates. He shall keep correct minutes of all proceedings of the Union, enter all receipts and expenditures, and countersign all orders that may be drawn upon the funds; he shall call special meetings when directed by the proper authority.

Sec. 2.—And it shall be his duty, in case of neglect or refusal of the President, to call a special meeting when requested so to do; to call such meeting when furnished with a written request signed by the Delegates of any three Societies.

Sec. 3.—He shall keep a correct list of the names and residence of the Delegates with the number of times each absents himself from the stated or special Meetings, together with all other defalcations, and shall deliver a written report of the same, with the amount of fines attached to each Delegate, to the Secretaries of their respective Societies at their next stated meeting.

Sec. 4.—He shall, at the expiration of his term of office, removal or resignation, deliver all books and effects he may have in his possession belonging to the Union, to his successor in office, when required so to do.

ARTICLE X.
Duties of the Coresponding Secretary.

Sec. 1.—It shall be the duty of the Corresponding Secretary to write all letters required by the Union, and upon the receipt of any letters or communications to lay the same before the next meeting.

Sec. 2.—In the absence of the Recording Secretary, his duties for the time being, shall devolve upon the Corresponding Secretary.

ARTICLE XI.
Duties of the Treasurer.

Sec. 1.—The Treasurer shall, at the discretion of the Union, hold funds to the amount of fifty dollars, for which he shall give such security as may be deemed sufficient, and no payment shall be made by him, without an order from the finance Committee, signed by the President, and countersigned by the Secretary of the Union.

Sec. 2.—He shall keep a correct account of all money by him received or paid; and his books shall at all times be open for the inspection of the Union, or a Committee thereof.

Sec. 3.—He shall, at the expiration of his term of office, removal or resignation, deliver all monies and effects belonging to the Union, to his successor in office, when required so to do.

ARTICLE XII.
Finance Comittee.

Sec. 1.—The Finance Committee shall consist of one member from each Society represented, to be appointed by such Society from the number of its Delegates, and no member of said Committee shall be eligible to any other office under this Constitution.

Sec. 2.—They shall each deliver to the President of this Union, at every stated meeting, the amount due from their respective Societies.

Sec. 3.—They shall dispense of the funds collected at

every stated meeting of the Union, in such manner as a majority of the societies present may direct.

Sec. 4.—They shall hold regular monthly meetings one week previous to each stated meeting of the Union, and shall present a correct report of the state of the funds, and of their proceedings at such stated meeting.

Sec. 5.—It shall be their duty to examine the Roll Books of each society represented at least once in three months, and report the number of members contained in each book, to the next stated meeting of the Union.

ARTICLE XIII.

The regular meeting of this Union shall be held on the third Tuesday in each month.

ARTICLE XIV.

Sec. 1.—Every Society represented in this Union shall pay at each stated meeting, into the funds thereof, the sum of 6 1-4 cents for each member of such society, and shall, on admission, pay one month's dues in advance.

Sec. 2.—Any represented society neglecting to pay its quota for two successive stated meetings shall be notified, and in case of neglect or refusal to pay at the stated meeting, shall forfeit all claims to the Union, and can only be readmitted on the terms of a new Society.

Sec. 3.—No orders whatever, shall be issued upon the funds, without the consent of the Union, expressed by a majority of Societies, at any stated or special meeting.

ARTICLE XV.

Sec. 1.—Any Society wishing to repel aggression, or desirous of striking for hours or wages, shall give written notice of the same to the President of the Union, who shall immediately direct the Secretary to call a special meeting, when the vote of two thirds of the Societies present shall be requisite to the granting of pecuniary assistance to any such represented society.

Sec. 2.—No Society shall be entitled to any pecuniary assistance from this Union, until it has been represented in the same for six months, and complied with all other constitutional requisites.

ARTICLE XVI.

Any Society wishing to be admitted in this Union, shall make application in writing to the Corresponding Secretary, who shall proceed according to Sec. 1. Art. 10 of this Constitution; an election by ballot shall then take place, and if a majority of the Union present consent, the society shall be entitled to representation, and the Corresponding Secretary shall, within three days, present a written notice of the same to either the President or Secretary thereof.

ARTICLE XVII.

Should any representative of a Society be found guilty of defrauding this Union in any manner, he shall be expelled, and not again admited—and the Society represented by him shall give such satisfaction as the Union may require.

ARTICLE XVIII.

No Political or religious question shall, at any time, be agitated in, or acted upon, by this Union, nor shall this Union, as an Association, at any time interfere with political concerns.

ARTICLE XIX.

All by-laws, in order to be valid, shall be sanctioned by a majority of the Societies present at any stated or special meeting.

ARTICLE XX.

Al vacancies that may occur in the Officers of this Union by removal, resignation or otherwise, shall be immediately filled by a new election.

ARTICLE XXI.

The election of Officers of this Union shall take place on the first stated meeting succeeding the appointment of Delegates, and the person receiving a majority of votes shall be declared duly elected.

ARTICLE XXII.

This Constitution may be amended or altered by receiving the sanction of a majority of delegates at any Regular meeting, and by being notified by two-thirds of the Societies here represented, four weeks notice having been given to the Union of such proposed alteration or amendment.

Newark, June 11th, 1834.

BY-LAWS.

RULES OF ORDER.

Rule 1.—As soon as the roll is called, the Recording Secretary shall read the minutes of the preceding meeting.

2.—The reading of credentials.

3.—Reports of Special Committees.

4.—Election of Officers.

5.—Report of the Finance Committee.

6.—Report of the Treasurer.

7.—Report of the Corresponding Secretary with Communications.

8.—Unfinished business.

9.—New propositions.

BY-LAWS.

Article 1.—At the hour of meeting the Recording Secretary shall call the roll, and if two-thirds of the Societies and Associations are each represented by one Delegate, it shall be a quorum, and the Convention shall proceed to business.

Article 2.—In the absence of an Officer, his place shall be filled *pro tem.*

Article 3.—As soon as the minutes are disposed of, a motion to adjourn shall always be in order.

Article 4.—No question shall be open for debate unless seconded, and no Member shall be allowed to speak more than twice on the same subject, unless it be by permission of the President, and then only by way of explanation; nor shall he be interrupted while speaking in order.

Article 5.—No motion shall be admitted by the President under a question of debate, unless it be to postpone the consideration thereof, to divide the question, or adjourns and no amendment shall be allowed that in the opinion of the President destroys the spirit of the matter under consideration.

Section 2.—No motion for reconsideration shall be received unless made by a member who voted in the affirmative.

Article 6.—Any Delegate that shall introduce Politics, or Religion, in this Union, shall, for the first offence receive a reprimand from the President, for the second, he shall pay a fine of 5 dollars, and for the third be expelled from the Union.

Article 7.—The Recording Secretary shall receive for his services one dollar for each regular or special meeting, and for each and every neglect of duty he shall pay a fine of one dollar.

Article 8.—Whenever a vacancy shall occur in any Delegation by death, resignation, or otherwise, it shall be filled only for the period said Delegate was elected.

Article 9.—All candidates for office shall be nominated by the finance Commitee, and balloted for, with written or printed ballots.

Section 2.—There shall be three Inspectors appointed to count the ballots, and inspect the election.

Article 10.—Any Delegate that absents himself from a meeting of the Union without a reasonable excuse, shall, for the first absence, pay a fine of 25 cents, for the second, 50 cents, and if absent the third, he shall be reported to the Society or Association he was elected to represent.

Section 2.—Any Officer that absents himself without a reasonable cause, shall pay a fine of one dollar.

Article 11.—Should any member refuse to come to order, when requested by the President, he shall, for the first offence, be fined one dollar, and for the second, expelled from the room for the evening.

Article 12.—Any member of the Finance Committee that neglects to attend a meeting of said Committee, shall pay a fine of one dollar, and no excuse, except sickness, be taken.

Article 13.—In all cases where the vote is taken by Societies, such voting shall be done by the Finance Committee.

APPENDIX B

CONSTITUTION OF THE FEDERATION OF TRADES AND
LABOR UNIONS OF NEW JERSEY, 1883

ARTICLE I. Name. This association shall be known as
the Federation of the Trades and Labor Unions of New
Jersey, and shall consist of such trades and labor unions
as shall, after being duly admtited, conform to its rules
and regulations and pay all contributions required to
carry out the objects of the Federation.

ARTICLE II. Objects. The objects of this Federation
shall be the encouragement and formation of trades and
labor unions: the encouragement and formation of amalgamated local trade or labor councils: the promotion of
state, national, and international trades and labor union
alliances: to secure state and national legislation favorable to the interests of the wage-working class.

ARTICLE III. Sessions. The sessions of the Federation
shall be held annually on the first Monday in October,
at such place as the delegates have elected at the preceding Congress.

ARTICLE IV. Representation. The basis of representation in the Congress of this Federation shall be: three
delegates for every *bona fide* trades or labor organization
represented.

ARTICLE V. Officers. At the annual sessions of this Federation the delegates shall elect a Legislative Committee,
consisting of seven delegates, one of whom shall be the
Federation Secretary, one the Federation Treasurer, and
one the President of the Congress.

ARTICLE VI. Duties of Officers. *Section 1.* The duties of the Legislative Commitee shall be to exercise a supervision over the organization and the execution of its laws and to carry out such instructions as may from time to time be given them at the sessions of this Federation.

Section 2. The Legislative commitee shall choose from among themselves a Chairman, First and Second Vice Chairmen for the ensuing year.

ARTICLE VII. Revenue. The revenue of this Federation shall be derived from a capitation tax of three cents per member annually from each Trades and Labor Union assembly or Council affiliated with the Federation, which tax shall be paid half yearly in advance to the Federation Secretary, by whom it shall be handed to the Treasurer.

ARTICLE VIII. Accounts. The accounts of the year shall be closed two weeks prior to the assembling of the congress and a balance sheet duly certified and presented to the same.

ARTICLE IX. Remuneration. The remuneration for loss of time by the Legislative Committee shall be at the rate of $3 *per diem;* travelling and incidental expenses to be also defrayed.

ARTICLE X. The Congress and the Political Parties. The annual Congress being simply and purely a convention of wage workers convened for their mutual interest and benefit and in no sense partisan purposes, the Federation declares that no resolution of a partisan character tending to endorse any of the political parties or their candidates shall be entertained, received, or acted upon by the Congress during its deliberations.

APPENDIX C

MEMBERSHIP OF THE NEW JERSEY STATE
FEDERATION OF LABOR, 1909-1956 *

Year	Membership	Year	Membership
1909	8,700	1927	21,200
1910	13,600	1928	38,700
1911	11,600	1929	36,000
1912	13,200	1930	36,700
1913	21,300		
1914	18,700	1931	34,400
		1932	28,400
1915	21,300	1933	
1916	18,700	1934	13,000
1917	25,700	1935	36,700
1918	21,900	1936	30,800
1919	21,900		
1920	31,600	1937	33,000
		1938	35,700
1921	25,800	1939	39,200
1922	25,400	1940	51,800
1923	27,900	1941	55,900
1924	27,600	1942	69,200
1925	29,200		
		1943	79,900
1926	27,700	1944	81,700

* Computed from annual per capita receipts of the N. J. State
Federation of Labor, AFL. From 1909 to 1950, the fiscal year of
the Federation was August 1 to July 31. The fiscal year was
changed to end March 31 at the 1951 Convention, so the fiscal
year ending March 31, 1952, corresponds to the year 1951 in the
table. 1957-1961, not available.

1945	86,500	1951	137,300
1946	88,700	1952	138,000
1947	93,200		
		1953	145,400
1948	88,700	1954	145,500
1949	88,400	1955	155,000
1950	126,300	1956	165,800

Miscellaneous Years

1890	1,700	1896	1,700
1893	1,000	1897	1,800
1895	2,000	1903	17,600

APPENDIX D

MEMBERSHIP OF THE NEW JERSEY STATE INDUSTRIAL UNION COUNCIL, 1941-1961 *

Year	Membership	Year	Membership
1941	52,500	1952	137,200
1942	93,600	1953	163,000
1943	121,900	1954	175,200
1944	193,100 **	1955	172,700
1945	151,600	1956	168,800
1946	116,100	1957	181,200
1947	159,800	1958	163,700
1948	135,000	1959	153,400
1949	119,500	1960	142,000
1950	110,300	1961 †	109,800
1951	129,300		

* Financial reports of the New Jersey State Industrial Council, 1942-1961. Figures computed from per capita receipts and rounded to the nearest hundred.

** Figure for eight months Oct. 1, 1943 to May 31, 1944.

† Figure is for eleven months.

CHART 1
NLRB REPRESENTATION ELECTIONS WON BY UNIONS IN NEW JERSEY, THE MIDDLE ATLANTIC STATES, AND THE UNITED STATES, 1946-1963

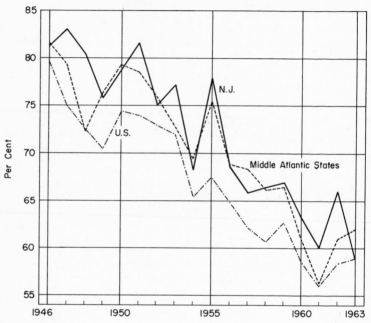

APPENDIX E

REPRESENTATION ELECTIONS WON BY UNIONS, NEW JERSEY, THE MIDDLE ATLANTIC REGION AND THE UNITED STATES, 1946-1963 *

(In percentages)

	1946	1947	1948	1949	1950	1951	1952	1953	1954	1955	1956	1957	1958	1959	1960	1961	1962	1963
United States	79.6	75	72.5	70.5	74.5	74	73	72	65.6	67.6	65.3	62.2	60.8	62.8	58.6	56.1	58.5	59.0
New Jersey	81.3	83.1	80.3	75.9	78.9	81.7	75.1	77.3	68.2	78	68.6	65.9	66.5	67	63.2	60	66.1	59.0
Middle Atlantic Region**	81.6	79.3	72.3	76.5	79.4	78.6	76	72.9	69.4	75.5	68.9	68.4	66.2	66.6	60.9	56.3	61	62.1

* National Labor Relations Board, *Annual Reports*, 1946-1963.

** Region includes New York, New Jersey and Pennsylvania.

CHART 2

NLRB ELECTION RESULTS BY UNION AFFILIATION IN NEW JERSEY, 1946-1963

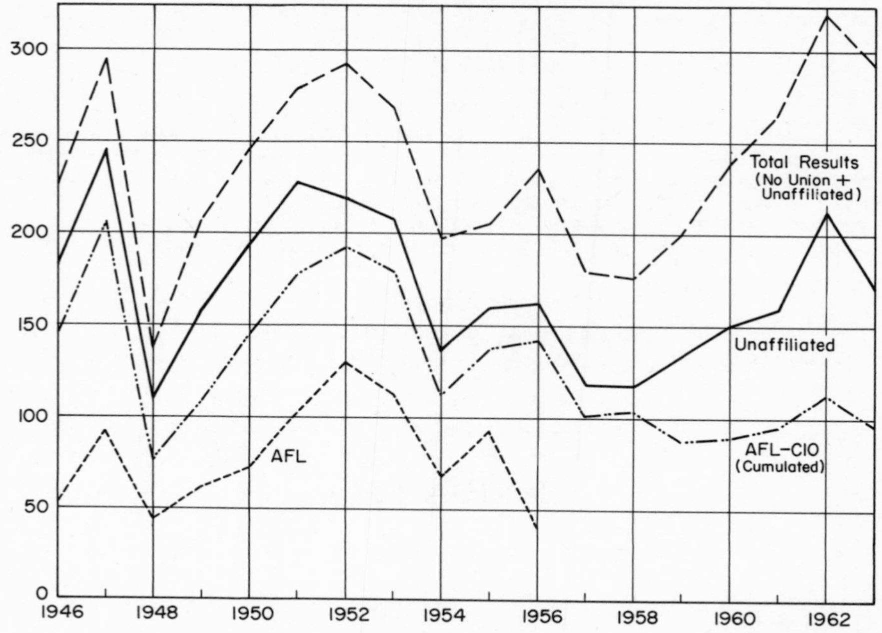

Total Results
(No Union +
Unaffiliated)

Unaffiliated

AFL–CIO
(Cumulated)

AFL

APPENDIX F

Representation Election Results by Union Affiliation in New Jersey, 1946-1963*

	1946	1947	1948	1949	1950	1951	1952	1953	1954	1955	1956	1957	1958	1959	1960	1961	1962	1963
A.F. of L.	53	94	44	61	72	102	130	114	68	94	40							
C.I.O.	93	112	33	48	73	76	63	66	45	43	43							
A.F.L.-C.I.O.											59	101	104	88	89	95	112	97
(Cumulated AFL-CIO)	146	206	77	109	145	178	193	180	113	137	142	101	104	88	89	95	112	97
Unaffiliated	37	39	33	48	49	50	27	28	23	23	20	17	13	46	62	64	100	76
(Cumulated AFL-CIO, Unaffiliated)	183	245	110	157	194	228	220	208	136	160	162	118	117	134	151	159	212	173
No Union	42	50	27	50	52	51	73	61	62	45	74	61	59	66	88	106	109	120
Total election results	225	295	137	207	246	279	293	269	198	205	236	179	176	200	239	265	321	293
Cumulated Percentage Distribution:																		
AFL	24	32	32	29	29	37	44	42	34	46								
AFL + CIO	65	70	56	53	59	64	66	67	57	67	60	56	59	44	37	36	35	33
AFL + CIO + Unaffiliated	81	83	80	76	79	82	75	77	69	78	69	66	66	67	63	60	66	59
Total	100	100	100	100	100	100	100	100	100	100	100	100	100	100	100	100	100	100

* National Labor Relations Board, *Annual Reports*, 1946-1963.

BIBLIOGRAPHICAL NOTES

CHAPTER I

An outstanding reference book is Eli Heckscher's, *Mercantilism* (London, 1962). For details on the organization of production and the separation of production functions in the United Kingdom prior to the Industrial Revolution, see George Unwin's classic, *Industrial Organization* (London, 1957). Also, E. Furniss, *The Position of the Laborer in a System of Nationalism* (New York, 1957). Richard B. Morris' scholarly treatise, *Government and Labor in Early America* (New York, 1946), provides comprehensive treatment of the application and decay of colonial-style mercantilism.

CHAPTER II

J. R. Commons' editorial *tours des forces, A Documentary History of American Industrial Society* (New York, 1958) and *History of Labor in the United States* (New York, 1946), are standard for detailed accounts of the development of unionism. Frank T. De Vyver's "The Organization of Labor in New Jersey Before 1860" (Unpublished doctoral dissertation, Princeton University, 1934) is the only work on the early history of unions in the State. It is rich in detail. Norman Ware's *The Industrial Worker, 1840-1860* (Gloucester, Mass., 1959) is an admirable and exceptionally competent analysis of labor organization for the period concerned. It is an excellent and a necessary complement to the Commons' publications.

CHAPTER III

Again, Commons' works must be accompanied by another book by Norman Ware, *The Labor Movement in the United States, 1860-1895* (New York, 1964), for a different perspective and an appreciation of the role of the Knights of Labor. The New Jersey Bureau of Statistics of Labor and Industry give valuable information and statistical data on the character of the New Jersey labor movement in the late nineteenth century. Particularly noteworthy is its *Tenth Annual Report, 1887.*

CHAPTER IV

A collection of information culled from newspapers and available proceedings of conventions dealing with the origin and development of the State Labor Congress, the State Federation of Organized Trades and Labor Unions, and the State Federation of Labor are to be found in the Special Collection of Rutgers University Library. The data are the work of Irvine Kerrison and associates.

James E. Wood's "History of Labor in the Broad Silk Industry of Paterson, New Jersey" (Unpublished doctoral dissertation, University of California, 1941) is an exceptionally valuable piece of research. It carefully and fully documents the development of unions in silk manufacturing in New Jersey from the late nineteenth century to the rise of the CIO.

For a detailed account of radical unionism's forays into woolen textiles in 1926, see Morton Siegel, "The Passaic Textile Strike of 1926" (Unpublished doctoral dissertation, Columbia University, 1953).

CHAPTER V

For additional material on the statistics of New Jersey unions, 1939-1953, see my article, "Union Membership in New Jersey," in *Review of New Jersey Business,* XII. Some of the organizational problems of the State Federation and the State CIO can be gleaned from available convention proceedings and officers' reports of these organizations.

CHAPTER VI

Martin Greenberg's "Injunctions in Labor Disputes in New Jersey," *Rutgers Law Review*, XI, is a critical review of the courts' application of New Jersey's Anti-Injunction Law. William M. Weinberg in "An Administrative History of the New Jersey State Board of Mediation" (Unpublished doctoral dissertation, University of Pennsylvania, 1964), provides an historical summary of mediation machinery in the State and a sympathetic presentation of the State Mediation Board's competition with the Federal Mediation and Conciliation Service.

The Department of Labor and Industry's Fiftieth Anniversary report in its *Summary of Activities, July 1, 1953–June 30, 1954* (Trenton, 1954) contains well-rounded synopses of New Jersey's principal labor and social legislation.

CHAPTER VII

W. C. Garrison's "The Negro in Manufacturing and Mechanical Industries," *Twenty-Sixth Annual Report of the Bureau of Labor and Industry of New Jersey, 1903* (Somerville, 1904), will give the reader an historical perspective on how little industry's and labor's practices toward Negroes has changed over the past six decades.

CHAPTER VIII

Allen Weisenfeld's "Collective Bargaining at the Crossroads," *Labor Law Journal*, June, 1963, brings the knowledge of a skilled and experienced New Jersey mediator and arbitrator to bear on the problems of contemporary bargaining.

INDEX

39n, 40n, 41, 47n, 48n, 50n, 51n, 52n, 55n, 60, 76n

New Jersey Committee for Democratic Trade Unionism, 125

N. J. CIO, 187

New Jersey CIO News, 184n, 190

New Jersey CIO Political Action Committee, 186, 191

New Jersey Department of Labor and Industry, 165n

New Jersey Gazette, Observation of "Rationalis," 16

New Jersey Industrial Union Council, 102, 200

New Jersey Labor Herald, 190, 191

New Jersey Labor Party, 184

New Jersey Reports, 143n

New Jersey Law Reports, 141n

New Jersey State Board of Mediation, 143, 157, 159, 160

New Jersey State Federation of Labor, AFL, 46, 59, 116, 121, 179; Convention Address by Hayes, John W. (1929), 54; Convention (1935), 117; Executive Board, 135; Origin, 52

New Jersey State Industrial Union Council, 138

New Jersey State Joint Board of TWOC, 108

New Jersey State Labor Congress, 141, 167

New Jersey State Labor Congress, 38, 55, 56, 57, 62, 63, 141, 167; As AFL Affiliate, 61; Became the Federation of Trades and Labor Unions of New Jersey, 38; Compared to Knights, 55-56; Hayes, John W., Founder, 53; New Jersey Federation of Trades and Labor Unions, 67; Product of Knights, 52; Simmerman,

Charles H. succeeded Hayes, 56

New Jersey Supreme Court, 143, 145, 145n, 177, 183; Superior Court (Chancery Division), 144

New Jersey Worsted, 95, 108

Newman, Philip C., 158n

New York Daily Graphic, 65n

New York State Parole Board, 188

New York Times, 115n, 117n, 133n, 138n, 185n, 197n, 199n, 200n

Noble, Ranson E. Jr., 161n, 180n

Norris, La Guardia Anti-Injunction Bill, 147, 162, 163

North American Phalanx, Headquarters Picture of, 33

North Jersey Joint Board, 110, 122

Nussbaum, Miriam, 144n

"Nutley Sun Printing" case, 144-145

Oil Workers, 113

Operating Engineers, 188

Organizing Committee, 105; of Rubbers Workers', 115; of Steel Workers', 114; of Telephone Workers', 112, 126; of Tetile Workers', 105, 106, 107, 108, 109, 110

Packinghouse Workers, 196

Painters, 40

Pancoast, Walter, 60

Parker, Joel, Governor, 42

Passaic Worsted, 95, 97

Patent Arms Mfg. Co., 78

Paterson Labor Bank, 91

Paterson Labor Standard, 66-67, 189

Paterson, W., 8n

Patrons of Husbandry Grange No. 9, 60